Shannon Trust Reading Programme

Turning Pages

The background
What is Turning Pages?

Welcome to Turning Pages.

Turning Pages has been developed specifically for adults, so that an adult who can read (the Mentor) uses it to support an adult who struggles with reading (the Learner).

How to use Turning Pages:

1) Read the introduction to each manual in full before starting with your Learner.

2) Make sure you are confident with the sounds by practising with the Sounds Charts on pages 5, 6 and 7 and phonic sounds audio file on the Shannon Trust website.

3) Read the Mentor pages for each activity and work though the manuals at a pace suitable for your Learner.

4) Introduce the Turning Pages reading books when prompted by the manuals and make sure Learners are able to choose which they want to read.

Turning Pages is made up of 5 manuals and 30 accompanying reading books and has been designed with the following rules in mind:

- Mentors follow the instructions in each manual and for each activity
- Learning is one-to-one
- 20-minute sessions take place 5 days a week
- Learning takes place in a suitable environment
- Learners always start at the beginning of the first manual

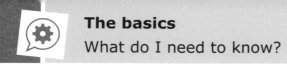

The basics

What do I need to know?

Turning Pages is phonic based and teaches reading in a logical sequence using manuals and accompanying reading books.

The phonic approach is about identifying the sounds within words and matching them to the letters of the alphabet that represent these sounds.

There are 44 sounds called **phonemes** in the English language. These are represented in written text by letters of the alphabet. There are only 26 letters in the alphabet with which to represent these 44 phonemes. So we use both single letters and groups of letters (graphemes) to represent all 44 phonemes.

There are three things to remember about the phonic approach to reading:

1. One sound (phoneme) can be represented by 1, 2, 3 or 4 letters (graphemes) such as:

1 letter	2 letters	3 letters	4 letters
c_a_t	**sh**_i_p	n_**igh**_t	th_**ough**

2. One sound can be represented by different combinations of letters, such as the **long ō** which can be written as:

    m**o**st   t**oe**   fl**oa**t   n**o**te   sl**ow**   th**ough**   s**ew**

The basics

What do I need to know?

3. One spelling can represent different sounds such as:

> f**ew** and s**ew,** pl**ough**, th**ough** and c**ough**

These phonic principles can seem hard. Turning Pages takes a structured approach which first introduces your Learner to a basic code where one letter = one sound.

These are the 44 sounds, colour coded to the Turning Pages manual they are covered in:

First Manual	Second Manual	Third Manual	Fourth Manual	Fifth Manual

Sound	Example	Example	Example	Example	Example
a	cat				
b	**b**un	ra**bb**it			
c	**c**ow	lu**ck**	**k**ite		
d	**d**og	a**dd**			
e	leg	h**ea**d			
f	**f**at	sti**ff**	**ph**one		
g	ba**g**	e**gg**			
h	**h**and				
i	in				
j	**j**ug	**gi**ant	he**dge**	**gy**rate	**gi**nger
l	**l**ip	fu**ll**			
m	**m**en	co**mm**a			
n	**n**ot	su**nn**y			

5

Sound	Example	Example	Example	Example	Example
o	pot				
p	hop	happy			
qu	quick				
r	rib	horrid			
s	sun	mess	city	race	cycle
t	top	potted			
u	run				
v	van				
w	win	when			
x (ks)	tax				
y	yes				
z	zip	jazz			
th	then	moth			
ch	chop	match			
sh	rush	station	session	musician	

Sound	Example	Example	Example	Example	Example	Example	Example	Example	Example
ng	ra**ng**								
nk	ra**nk**								
zh	televi**si**on								
(Long) ā	r**ai**n	d**ay**	t**a**me	**ei**ght	th**ey**	gr**ea**t	**a**ble		
(Long) ē	tr**ee**	t**ea**	ver**y**	**e**ve	reli**e**f	k**ey**	m**e**	rec**ei**ve	ser**i**ous
(Long) ō	b**oa**t	gr**ow**	n**o**te	t**oe**	th**ough**	**o**pen	s**ew**		
(Long) ī	m**y**	f**igh**t	l**i**ke	t**ie**	v**i**rus	h**ei**ght			
(Long) ū	sh**oo**t	b**oo**k	c**ue**	f**ew**	t**u**be	s**ou**p	d**o**	s**u**per	s**ui**t
ar	c**ar**d								
er	lett**er**	b**ur**n	b**ir**d	col**our**	doct**or**	**ear**th	coll**ar**		
ow	h**ou**se	c**ow**							
oi	s**oi**l	b**oy**							
or	f**or**	m**ore**	y**aw**n	fr**au**d	b**oar**d	d**oor**	th**ough**t	w**ar**m	c**our**t
ul	hand**le**	med**al**	skilf**ul**	petr**ol**	funn**el**	ev**il**			
air	h**air**	b**are**	w**ear**						
chur	pic**ture**								

7

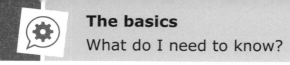

The basics
What do I need to know?

The manuals are structured so that you work through them page by page, activity by activity. Always start at the beginning of the first manual with a new Learner and work your way through to make sure there are no gaps in their phonic knowledge. **Don't be tempted to skip activities or pages**.

The two facing pages always work together: the left-hand page is for you (the Mentor) and the right-hand page is for your Learner. The Mentor page is explained opposite.

Whenever you are working with your Learner keep these things in mind:
- Use letter sounds not the names of the letters.
- Keep the alphabet charts handy for reference.
- At the start of each session revisit the last page you did with your Learner.
- Use the Notes box to carry over anything your Learner has struggled with or found difficult and go over these again (on that day and/or at the next session). Use the Parking pages to note down words or sounds that need even more practice.
- When your Learner is ready, give them the opportunity to do the writing and ticking.
- Adjust the pace of learning to your Learner's needs:
  - Do not rush them through the activities. Repeat them as many times as seems necessary.
  - Be prepared to progress quickly if your Learner is clearly coping with the tasks. Do not skip any activities though.
- Give your Learner loads of praise – however, be honest and constructive about any difficulties.

The Mentor page
What does it all mean?

Words to read
This box lists all the words you need to read to your Learner. It also shows how to sound them out.

Sometimes this box will show **Words to find** in gap fill and word build activities.

Heading
This shaded box gives you the title of the activity and what your Learner will do to develop their reading skills.

This box gives you numbered instructions for each activity. Make sure you do each part of the activity in the order given.

Italics
Words or letters written in italics mean that they should be sounded out.

 Listen and point

Learners match sounds to the letters they see

Words to read
1. sat   *s-a-t*
2. it   *i-t*
3. tin   *t-i-n*
4. pat   *p-a-t*
5. an   *a-n*
6. tap   *t-a-p*
7. in   *i-n*
8. nip   *n-i-p*

Tip: Your Learner may prefer you to write for them. Ask them to point to each letter and say its sound.

Learning to blend sounds to make words is a vital skill for reading so it is important you say the letter sounds correctly.

1. Ask your Learner to read the **sounds** at the top of the Learner page: **s**, **a**, **i**, **p**, **t** and **n**
   • Explain that you are going to put these sounds together to make words.

2. Tell your Learner to listen to the sounds.
   • Read out the first word: **sat**
   • Point to each letter as you sound out the word sat: *s-a-t*
   • Read out the whole word again showing how the letters blend.
   • Write the letters in the boxes and the word **sat** on the line.

3. Read out the second word to your Learner and sound it out letter-by-letter: **it**/*i-t*
   • Ask your Learner to point to each letter as you say the sound.
   • Invite your Learner to write the letters in the boxes, if they are not ready to write, do it for them. Read the whole word again to show how the letters blend.

4. Do the same for each of the other words.
   • Explain that a handwritten **a** is usually different to a printed **a**. Show this in your own handwriting.

Notes:

Tip:
Sometimes there will be some tips. These are suggestions that will help you to support your Learner.

Notes:
This is your space to:
• Make a note of any words or sounds that your Learner needs to practise again.
• Keep track of progress.
• Jot down anything that is useful to **you**!

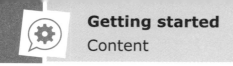

Getting started
Content

Make sure you are confident with the sounds you will be doing before you start.

The first part of this manual forms the basis of all other learning in the programme. It is worth spending plenty of time to get it right. Be prepared to repeat activities until your Learner is really confident. Your Learner needs to learn all the letter sounds including **sh**, **ch**, and **th**. These are shown on the alphabet chart. They may well know the names of the letters but they should not use them and must learn and practise the **sound** that each letter represents.

- It is important that your Learner learns to listen for sounds. Your pronunciation of each sound will be very important.
- Your Learner needs to recognise that single letters sound the same whether they are in capital letters or lower case.
- Your Learner will **blend** sounds together to make words. This is a key skill for reading.
- Your Learner will also learn some Sight Words, such as **the**, **to** and **he**, by sight and read short sentences.
- Later in the programme your Learner will learn that different letter combinations are used to make other sounds, such as **ee**, **ay** and **igh** but at this stage you need to make sure that your Learner makes a clear link between the letter and the sound it represents.

Getting started
Sight Words

The English language contains a number of words that are used time and time again. These are called high frequency words. Some of these words are phonically regular and can be easily decoded, such as **on**, **did** and **him** but others do not work so well with phonics and need to be learned as whole words such as **the**, **some**, **one**, **said** and **all**. **These will be described as Sight Words in Turning Pages**. You will need to explain this to your Learner when you get to Sight Words in this manual.

Sight Words are essential to reading even at the earliest stages. It is important that some of them are introduced early on so that your Learner can read sentences and longer texts. Sight Words will be introduced gradually throughout Turning Pages. Your Learner will need plenty of practice to make sure they can easily recognise and read them as whole words. Some Learners find it helpful to take a picture of the word in their head.

Sight Words covered in this manual		
the	what	no
to	have	go
I	you	they
was	for	all
he	of	put
she	do	I'm
me	are	could
be	my	would
we	time	there
	out	day
	about	don't
		her

To make it easier to read longer words, Learners need to break them down into smaller 'chunks' called syllables and then put them back together again to build the whole word.

These 'chunks' are the beats that can be tapped out when a word is read aloud.

Words can be **one syllable** (one beat) long such as: **bed, reach, know, dressed**, or have **two, three, four,** or **more** syllables such as: **to/day, fan/tas/tic, diff/i/cul/ty, org/an/i/sa/tion.** It doesn't matter too much where a Learner puts the break as long as they get the number of syllables right and each syllable has a vowel.

Mentors can help their Learners by:

- Reading longer words aloud slowly, tapping out each syllable as they say it: **fan/tas/tic** (three beats)
- Telling their Learner that every syllable has a vowel sound in it. This may be a single vowel: **a, e, i, o, u** (**y** can also be a vowel) or a vowel sound made from letter combinations such as: ***ai, ay, ee, ea, or, ar, aw, igh, air***
- Getting them to try the **V**owel, **S**ound, **B**reak (VSB) method with longer words. This method asks the learner to find the **V**owel sound (there may be more than one); then the letter **S**ound that follows it and to then mark in the syllable **B**reak (forward slash /) after this sound. This works with words such as: pan/ic, con/tain, wis/dom, ad/ven/ture
- Telling them to keep double letters together as one sound such as: rabb/it, miss/ing
- Uncovering a longer word a bit at a time from left to right, reading each 'chunk' as it appears.

If a Learner is having a particular problem with what is a 'b' and what is a 'd' here are some things you can try with them:

- Put a 'b' in the left hand corner and a 'd' in the right hand corner of each Turning Pages page and practise these at the start of each session. Keep referring to the 'b' and d' when reading the words on the page.

- Have a b/d prompt card on the desk. e.g

- Use a hand prompt for 'b' and 'd'. You can show the Learners how to do this and they can even write the b' and 'd' on their hands, as in the picture. Then they can look at their left hand for a 'b' and their right hand for a 'd'. It sounds a bit mad but it sometimes helps!

- Use the prompt of a bat and ball for 'b'.

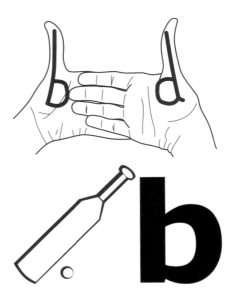

- Use the prompt of 'cd' (as in compact disk) to show that 'd' follows 'c' and is also formed with 'c' as the basis.

- These prompts can help with letter formation as well as letter recognition.

- Remember that the b/d section on page 40 of the first Turning Pages manual can be practised regularly. It might be useful to include 3 or 4 words for practice at every session, perhaps as a starting exercise. However, one Mentor found it useful to use the page mid-session or sometimes at the end, when the Learner had relaxed.

Writing
Supporting Learners with writing

Turning Pages invites Learners to do the writing on the Learner Page. You should encourage your Learner to write but don't force them until they are ready.

Remember the written *a* is different in shape to the most commonly used printed **a.**

Our primary focus is on reading so we do not look at formally teaching writing skills but there are a few things so watch out for:

- If you do the writing for your Learner in the early stages use lower-case letters
- Don't use joined–up writing
- Write as big as the space allows
- Be clear

When Learners are writing:

- Don't criticise how they do it
- Make sure they are holding the pencil comfortably
- Encourage them to use lower-case letters
- If they spell something wrong praise the effort and then show them the correct spelling, pointing out the sounds

Only use the How to Form Letters sheet (see following page) to help them practise if your Learner really struggles with forming the letters.

Writing
How to form letters

If your Learner is struggling with forming letters you may want to refer to the chart below for guidance.

Remember the written *a* is different in shape to the commonly printed **a**.

a b c d e f g

h i j k l m n

o p q r s t u

v w x y z

Turning Pages
Reading books and supported reading

As soon as your Learner reaches the first Progress Check in Turning Pages you should introduce them to the relevant reading books. It's important that you encourage your Learners to start reading real texts as soon as they are able.

What to read

Turning Pages reading books have been developed specifically for this purpose.

Learners should be able to choose which book they want to read from the level they have reached but don't be tempted to skip ahead and offer some of the other books as they won't have learned the skills needed yet. Each reading book lists which level they are aimed at inside the front cover.

Learners can tackle the Turning Pages reading books on their own but it is important to do this only when your Learner feels ready (and after you have gone through the Out of Level words). For the less confident Learner supported reading is a simple method that enables the Learner to safely practise all the reading skills needed to develop fluency.

When to read

- Following each Progress Check, have the relevant Turning Pages reading books with you to look at with your Learner.
- Include all the Turning Pages reading books they can choose from for example if they have reached the end of the second manual, have all the Turning Pages reading books up to that point available. They may want to re-read one they have read before or they may not have read them all previously.
- Look at the Turning Pages reading books, help your Learner to read the titles and the blurb on the back of the books and discuss them. Encourage your Learner to pick one they would like to read.

Turning Pages

Reading books and supported reading

- Open the book at the page which shows the Out of Level words and go through these with your Learner – show them the word, read the word out to them, ask them to read it (help out if they need it) and then you read it out again. Make sure they know what the word means. Move on to the next word and don't rush.
- If your Learner then takes the book away to read on their own make sure they bring it to the next session so you can discuss how they are getting on, help with any bits they may have got stuck on and any word meanings they didn't know (if any).
- Have a discussion on what the book is about and how they feel about it. Be encouraging, if they didn't like the book, praise them on their effort to read it and help them choose another. If they give up on a book, it may be worth reading it with them as outlined below.

What to do

In the early days (particularly in the first two manuals) your Learner may not feel ready to take a reading book away and tackle it on their own straight away. To help them you can do some supported reading with them as follows:

- Supported reading is about reading for fluency and understanding so it is important that you don't insist your Learner 'sounds out' new words. Many Learners will happily attempt to sound out new words, which is fine as long as fluency and comprehension are not compromised.

Stage One – Discussion

Find out what your Learner thinks about the book and what it might be about based on the title and the pictures inside.

At the start of the book you will see a list of words which you will need to go over with your Learner before you start as described in the section above. Some of these will be social Sight Words (words that appear a lot in public places such as taxi) and others may be words they need for the story but have not yet been covered in Turning Pages.

Turning Pages

Reading books and supported reading

Stage Two – Read together

1. Ensure you both have a clear view of the text. Read some of the text aloud, pointing to each word as you say it.

2. Read the pages again, still pointing but ask your Learner to read along too. Adjust your speed to your Learner's speed.

3. Read the text together again but every line omit to speak a word so that your Learner says it without your voice. Choose words you know your Learner can read. As they become more confident you can withdraw more of your spoken words.

4. When ready, your Learner reads the text on their own and you give only the words that they pause at. Always wait 2 to 3 seconds for your Learner to work it out before you give the word. Don't force your Learner to sound it out – always give the word to maintain fluency.

5. Discuss what you have read.

6. Remember to give appropriate and specific praise.

It is important to be FLEXIBLE. A very inexperienced Learner may need to go through all 6 stages as laid out above but as confidence increases stages 1 and 2 could be gradually omitted.

Feel free to read other suitable things with your Learner if they are keen – tabloid newspapers can be an easy read for emergent readers.

You can find more help and information on Turning Pages on the Shannon Trust website including:

- An audio file where you can listen to and practise the sounds chart.

- An audio file where your Learner can listen to and practise the first sounds covered in Turning Pages.

- An audio file with some Top Tips for Mentors.

- A 'letter cards' template.

- Completion certificates.

Get started

1. Use the statements on the opposite page to explain to your Learner what they will be learning in this manual.

2. Explain that you will be working through each activity step by step from start to finish even if your Learner already has some knowledge. This will ensure that there are no gaps in their knowledge.

3. Stress that the skills introduced in these first few pages are the most important part of learning to read. They may take some time.

4. Explain that Turning Pages uses the **sounds** of the letters to build up their reading skills and so even though they may know the names of the letters of the alphabet, you will not be using them here.

In this manual you will:

Match sounds to their letters.

Practise all the letter sounds.

Begin to blend letter sounds together to make short words.

Sound out words.

Begin to read some words by sight.

Begin to read short sentences.

Start to move on to reading longer words.

You will be asked to **listen**, **look** and **read** aloud.

You can also have a go at writing short words.

There will be lots of chances for you to see how you are getting on and the progress you are making.

Listen and point

Learners identify sounds using the alphabet chart

This activity is the foundation of all phonic learning. It is essential that **only letter sounds** are referred to, **not letter names**.

1. Explain to your Learner that although letters have names it is very important to learn and use the letter sounds and not the letter names. Explain that some sounds are made by more than one letter, such as **sh**, **th** and **ch**.

2. Point to each picture in the alphabet chart and say the word that it represents. Ask your Learner to say the word after you. Make sure they know the right word for each picture and get the sound right.

3. Point to each picture in order, asking your Learner to say the whole word and then to say the initial sound: **apple, a**
   • Repeat this until your Learner is able to say each of the sounds correctly.

4. Point to the pictures in random order. Ask your Learner to say the initial sound and then the whole word: **a apple**. Remember the **c** sound can be made by the **c**, **k** and **ck** letters.

5. Say random single letter sounds and ask your Learner to point to the correct pictures and letters.
   • Point out that **x** sounds as **ks** as in fox and tax. It normally occurs at the end of words.

Tip: Ask your Learner if they can think of any other words that begin with the same sounds as you go through the alphabet.

Notes:

Listen and point
Start to read by learning the letter sounds

a **A** apple	**b** **B** bed	**c** **C** cake	**d** **D** dice	**e** **E** egg
f **F** fork	**g** **G** gate	**h** **H** hand	**i** **I** information	**j** **J** jug
k **K** keys	**l** **L** ladder	**m** **M** mouse	**n** **N** neck	**o** **O** octopus
p **P** pen	**qu** **Qu** queen	**r** **R** razor	**s** **S** sun	**t** **T** table
u **U** umbrella	**v** **V** van	**w** **W** web	**x** **X** box	**y** **Y** yo-yo
z **Z** zip	**ch** chair	**sh** shower	**th** thumb **th** the	**ck** sock

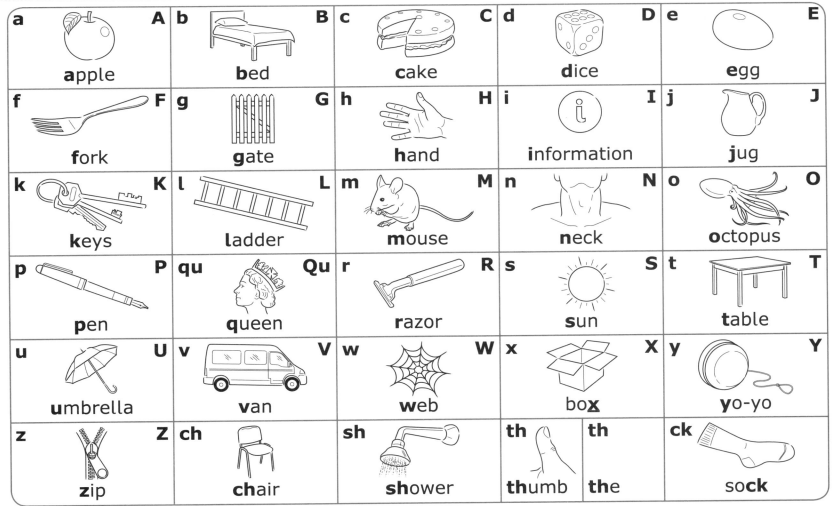

25

Read and check

Learners recognise the sounds that letters represent

1. Remind your Learner that they are learning letter **sounds** not letter names. Refer to the alphabet chart again if needed.

2. Ask your Learner to sound out each letter or letter combination, such as **sh**, **ch** and **th** in the grid. This also includes **qu**.
   - Tick the ones they get right. Your Learner can do this if they feel confident enough to write themselves.
   - Leave the others blank.

3. When your Learner has finished, go over any letters that have not been ticked.
   - Use the alphabet chart to go over the sounds they are not sure of until they are confident.
   - Make a note of any letters that your Learner finds difficult in the Notes box. There will be many opportunities for them to practise these in the following activities.

Tip: Use other pictures or familiar names to reinforce the recognition of sounds.

Notes:

Read and check
Check that you know the letter sounds

	✓
a	
w	
t	
k	
n	
o	
e	
b	
h	
f	
ch	
j	
p	
l	
m	
g	
v	
sh	
y	

	✓
s	
a	
t	
u	
d	
z	
th	
b	
e	
s	
g	
u	
i	
r	
c	
qu	
v	
x	
th	

	✓
ck	
d	
h	
r	
i	
p	
c	
w	
l	
f	
sh	
x	
a	
y	
ch	
o	
m	
j	
n	

Listen and point

Learners listen for sounds and then match them to letters

1. Ask your Learner to listen to the first sound in each word that you say.
- Remind them that some sounds can be made by more than one letter such as: **sh**, **ch** and **th**.

2. Say the word: **mouse**. Point to **m** in the chart opposite. Tell your Learner that this letter represents the first sound of the word mouse: **m**.

3. Say any word from the chart on page 25 at random.
- Do not show your Learner the alphabet chart with the pictures on page 25 at this stage.
- Using the chart opposite, ask your Learner to point to the letter that represents the first sound of each word that you say.
- Say the word again.
- Repeat this process with all the sounds until you are happy your Learner is confident with them – focus on any you made a note of at the end of the last activity.
- Use the alphabet chart with pictures if your Learner needs the extra support.
- Point out that the sounds *ck* and *x* are not found at the beginning of words.

Tip: You can practise the **x** sound (*ks*) using words such as **box**, **fox**, **tax** and **mix**.

Notes:

Listen and point

Listen for the first sound in words

a A	b B	c C	d D	e E
f F	g G	h H	i I	j J
k K	l L	m M	n N	o O
p P	qu Qu	r R	s S	t T
u U	v V	w W	y Y	z Z
sh	ch	th	th	ck x X

29

1. Look at the alphabet chart with the pictures on page 25.
   - Explain that **c**, **k** and **ck** make the same sound.

2. Ask your Learner to sound out each letter or letter combination in the grid on the page opposite.
   - Tick the ones they get right and leave the others blank.
   - Encourage your Learner to do the ticks.

3. Make a note of any letters that are still a problem.
   - Go over these letters again once or twice.
   - If any letter remains a problem, or takes two or three tries to get right, spend some more time working with the alphabet chart before moving on.

Tip:

Notes:

Read and check
Check that you know the letter sounds

	✓
ck	
f	
l	
a	
n	
s	
u	
j	
ch	
z	
th	
v	
d	
s	
t	
x	
m	
e	
p	

	✓
h	
o	
y	
u	
ck	
b	
i	
d	
g	
m	
sh	
w	
n	
k	
r	
c	
l	
j	
o	

	✓
v	
f	
ck	
i	
a	
p	
r	
ch	
c	
h	
s	
qu	
g	
sh	
e	
y	
b	
th	
w	

31

Listen and point

Learners match capital letters to lower case letters

1. Look at the alphabet chart again and point to the **capital letters** and explain to your Learner that:
   - The sound they represent is the same whether it is a capital letter or not.
   - Capital letters are used for names such as people, places, book names, TV programmes and they are also used at the beginning of sentences.
   - The other letters are called **lower case** letters.
   - Some capital letters look very different from the lower case letter, such as **G** and **g**.

2. Say the letter sound *g* and point to it in the lower case box.
   - Find the capital letter **G** in the bottom box.
   - Copy the capital letter **G** into the box under the lower case **g**.
   - Encourage your Learner to do the writing if they feel happy to do this.

3. Repeat the activity with all the other letters.

Tip: It is usually easier to read text in lower case letters because they have more shape, such as: help and HELP.

Notes:

Listen and point
Match capital letters to lower case letters

lower case letters																										
g	o	e	m	a	t	f	n	b	u	k	p	r	c	w	l	i	v	qu	j	d	s	y	h	z	x	

A	B	C	D	E	F	G	H	I	J	K	L	M	N	O	P	Qu	R	S	T	U	V	W	X	Y	Z
CAPITAL LETTERS																									

Read and check

Learners read letter sounds including those represented by capital letters

1. Ask your Learner to sound out each letter or letter combination in the grid on the opposite page.
   - Tick the ones they get right.
   - Encourage your Learner to do the ticks.
   - Leave the others blank.

2. When your Learner has finished, go over any letters that have not been ticked.
   - Use the alphabet chart if needed.

3. Make a note in the Notes box of any letters that your Learner still finds difficult. Go over these again once or twice before moving on.

Tip: Use some everyday text from a newspaper or a poster and ask your Learner to pick out some capital letters.

Notes:

Read and check
Check that you know the letter sounds including capital letters

	✓
r	
d	
N	
g	
e	
L	
t	
o	
K	
C	
f	
S	
H	
j	
W	
m	
u	
M	
ck	

	✓
a	
ck	
V	
I	
l	
sh	
s	
p	
k	
J	
ch	
G	
T	
i	
h	
D	
Z	
v	
N	

	✓
th	
A	
b	
Qu	
Y	
f	
R	
qu	
B	
F	
n	
y	
U	
E	
c	
J	
O	
P	
w	

Listen and count

Learners identify the number of sounds in words

Words to read

1. shop   *sh-o-p* (3)
2. on   *o-n* (2)
3. fish   *f-i-sh* (3)
4. cat   *c-a-t* (3)
5. sock   *s-o-ck* (3)
6. lost   *l-o-s-t* (4)
7. spit   *s-p-i-t* (4)
8. chat   *ch-a-t* (3)

Tip: It may help your Learner to tap out the sounds: one tap for each sound.

1. Ask your Learner to listen for letter sounds.
   - Read out the first word **shop** from the **Words to read** box. Then sound out the word: ***sh-o-p*** (3 sounds)
   - On the Learner page, circle the correct number to show the number of sounds.
   - Write the word for your Learner and sound it out again pointing to the letters or letter combinations that make each sound.

2. Read the second word to your Learner and then sound it out: **on/o-n**
   - Ask your Learner to circle the number of **sounds** they can hear in the word (2).
   - Ask your Learner what sounds they heard. Write the word for your Learner and sound it out again.
   - Do the same for each of the other words.
   - Point out the words where two letters represent one sound, such as fi**sh**, so**ck** and **ch**at.

3. This activity is not about spelling, so it is best that you do the writing for your Learner.

Notes:

Listen and count
Count the number of sounds you hear in each word

	The number of sounds				The whole word
1.	1	2	③	4	_____
2.	1	2	3	4	_____
3.	1	2	3	4	_____
4.	1	2	3	4	_____
5.	1	2	3	4	_____
6.	1	2	3	4	_____
7.	1	2	3	4	_____
8.	1	2	3	4	_____

Listen and point

Learners match sounds to the letters they see

Words to read

1. sat   *s-a-t*
2. it   *i-t*
3. tin   *t-i-n*
4. pat   *p-a-t*
5. an   *a-n*
6. tap   *t-a-p*
7. in   *i-n*
8. nip   *n-i-p*

Tip: Your Learner may prefer you to write for them. Ask them to point to each letter and say its sound.

Learning to blend sounds to make words is a vital skill for reading so it is important you say the letter sounds correctly.

1. Ask your Learner to read the **sounds** at the top of the Learner page: *s*, *a*, *i*, *p*, *t* and *n*.
   - Explain that you are going to put these sounds together to make words.

2. Tell your Learner to listen to the sounds.
   - Read out the first word: **sat**
   - Point to each letter as you sound out the word sat: ***s-a-t***
   - Read out the whole word again showing how the letters blend.
   - Write the letters in the boxes and the word **sat** on the line.

3. Read out the second word to your Learner and sound it out letter by letter: ***it/i-t***
   - Ask your Learner to point to each letter as you say the sound.
   - Invite your Learner to write the letters in the boxes. If they are not ready to write, do it for them. Read the whole word again to show how the letters blend.

4. Do the same for each of the other words.
   - Explain that a handwritten ***a*** is usually different to a printed **a**. Show this in your own handwriting when you write out the words.

Notes:

s a i p t n

1. ☐☐☐   = _____

2. ☐☐   = _____

3. ☐☐☐   = _____

4. ☐☐☐   = _____

5. ☐☐   = _____

6. ☐☐☐   = _____

7. ☐☐   = _____

8. ☐☐☐   = _____

Listen and point

Learners focus on reading letters **b** and **d** with confidence

Words to read

dug	dad
bin	lid
rod	bash
bag	cub
red	den
dash	rob
bed	cab
bill	bad
bog	dog

Tip: Using a hands-on approach is the best way to help your Learner. There is some more help on this on pages 13 and 14 of this manual.

1. Explain to your Learner that the two letters **b** and **d** can be easily mixed up because they are the same shape but in reverse.

2. Ask your Learner to point to the big letter: **b** on the Learner page and say its sound: **b**
   - Suggest that they use a finger or pencil to trace over the letter several times each time repeating the sound: **b**. Tell them that we learn many things well if we actually use our hands to do it, such as in car repairs. If they are not keen to do this then do not push the point.

3. Read each word in the left-hand box with your Learner emphasising the **b** in each word.

4. Repeat the process with the letter **d**.

5. Now read out the words in the **Words to read** box one at a time. Ask your Learner to listen and find the word in the list. Tell them to tick it when they find it.

Notes:

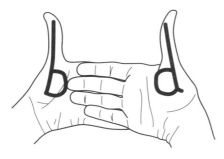

b

dug	dog
bag	lid
bog	dad
cub	bad
bed	bin
rob	red
den	bash
rod	cab
dash	bill

d

bat

beg

bin

big

but

we**b**

dog

dash

den

duck

dim

re**d**

41

Read and check

Learners practise reading two and three-letter words

1. Ask your Learner to read each word in the grid on the Learner page.
   - Tick all the words they get right and leave the others blank.

2. When your Learner has finished, go over any words that have not been ticked.
   - Read each of these words and sound them out letter by letter.
   - Then ask your Learner to read them again and tick the ones they get right.

3. Make a note, in the Notes box, of any words that are still a problem. Go over these words once or twice.

4. If any words remain a problem, or take two or three tries to get right, add them to the blank column on page 47. Your Learner can practise them again when you reach that page.

Tip: Use the alphabet charts to support your Learner if needed.

Notes:

Read and check
Check that you can read short words

	✓
win	
man	
in	
net	
at	
kit	
bag	
hit	
fin	
can	
jug	
pop	
leg	
gun	
got	
on	
rib	

	✓
sun	
dig	
tug	
van	
den	
zip	
tax	
bob	
wet	
it	
red	
pet	
hut	
rob	
tap	
up	
hen	

Listen

Learners listen and identify the order of sounds in spoken words

Words to read

1. rat   *r-a-t*
2. bed   *b-e-d*
3. tip   *t-i-p*
4. hot   *h-o-t*
5. van   *v-a-n*
6. cup   *c-u-p*
7. wet   *w-e-t*
8. rich   *r-i-ch*

Tip: The sounds *o* and *u* are easily confused, so be very clear when you sound out the words **hot** and **cup**.

1. Read out the first word: **rat**
   - Sound out the word clearly: ***r-a-t***
   - Ask your Learner:
     - What is the first sound you can hear? ***r***
     - What is the middle sound? ***a***
     - What is the last sound you can hear? ***t***
   - Write the separate letters in the spaces on the Learner page.
   - Say the whole word again blending the sounds. Write the whole word.

2. Repeat the steps above for each word in the **Words to read** box.
   - Ask your Learner to listen and identify each sound in the words.
   - Use the alphabet on the Learner page to find the correct letters for each sound.
   - Ask your Learner to write the letters in the spaces and then to write the whole word.
   - Explain to your Learner that they don't need to worry about handwriting or punctuation.

Notes:

a b c d e f g h i j k l m n o p qu r s t u v w x y z sh ch th ck

	r a t	rat
1.	__ __ __	_____
2.	__ __ __	_____
3.	__ __ __	_____
4.	__ __ __	_____
5.	__ __ __	_____
6.	__ __ __	_____
7.	__ __ __	_____
8.	__ __ __	_____

Read and check

Learners read more two and three-letter words

1. Tell your Learner that this is an opportunity for them to practise reading short words.
  • Ask your Learner to read each word in the grid on the Learner page.
  • Tick all the words they get right and leave the others blank.

2. When your Learner has finished, go over any words that have not been ticked.
  • Read each word, sound it out letter by letter and then ask your Learner to read it again.

3. Make a note of any words that are still a problem, or take two or three tries to get right, in the blank column on page 51. Your Learner can practise them again when you reach that page.

Tip: Use the alphabet charts to support your Learner if needed.

Notes:

Read and check
Check that you can read short words

	✓
pen	
cap	
on	
not	
it	
pip	
as	
hit	
ten	
ran	
jug	
kit	
log	
fan	
got	
up	
wig	

	✓
sun	
dug	
run	
van	
wet	
zip	
fox	
men	
bet	
in	
leg	
quit	
yes	
sex	
sad	
at	
ham	

Words from page 43	✓

Gap fill

Learners use vowels to complete words

Words to find

1. map mop
2. cat cot cut
3. rib rob rub
4. ban Ben bin bun
5. fan fen fin fun
6. bat bet bit but

Tip: Point out that names (as in Ben) have a capital letter.

1. Ask your Learner to read the sounds at the top of the Learner page: *a*, *e*, *i*, *o* and *u*.
   - Explain that these letters are called **vowels** and are in most words.

2. Ask your Learner to look at the first incomplete word on the list: **m _ p**
   - Show that by trying out all the letters you can make the words **map** and **mop**. Make sure that you try **all** the letters (vowels) but explain that mip, mup or mep are not real words.
   - Write in the missing letters to make **map** and **mop**.

3. Ask your Learner to do the same with the other words using each vowel in turn.
   - Encourage your Learner to write in the letters.
   - Discuss any non-words that they may come up with. Praise their phonic skills but make sure they only complete the real words.
   - The number of gapped words on the page shows how many real words can be made. Names such as Ben are fine.

Notes:

Gap fill
Use vowels to complete words

| | a e i o u | | |

1. m __ p   m __ p

2. c __ t   c __ t   c __ t

3. r __ b   r __ b   r __ b

4. b __ n   B __ n   b __ n   b __ n

5. f __ n   f __ n   f __ n   f __ n

6. b __ t   b __ t   b __ t   b __ t

Read and check

Learners read more words including those with **sh**, **ch**, **th** and **ck**

1. Remind your Learner that more than one letter can represent a single sound such as:
sh, **ch**, **th** and **ck**.

2. Ask your Learner to read each word in the grid on the Learner page.
- Tick all the words they get right and leave the others blank.
- When your Learner has finished, go over any words that have not been ticked.
- Read each word, sound it out and then read it again.

3. Ask your Learner to read them again and tick those they get right.

4. Make a note of any words that are still a problem, or take two or three tries to get it right, on the Parking page (page 65). Your Learner can practise them again when you reach that page.

Tip: Use the alphabet charts to support your Learner if needed. Use your finger to uncover one word at a time. This will help your Learner to focus on each word.

Notes:

Read and check
Check again that you can read short words

	✓
bag	
peg	
win	
dog	
sob	
fan	
vet	
hit	
jog	
lid	
mum	
nut	
hop	
quid	
ram	
yet	

	✓
fig	
rock	
bug	
bit	
an	
let	
that	
chop	
dash	
much	
luck	
up	
rich	
them	
lack	
mug	

	✓
thin	
posh	
sick	
chin	
tin	
wish	
shed	
gash	
such	
fish	
wag	
fun	
thud	
shot	
fed	
back	

Words from page 47	✓

Word build

Learners make two or three-letter words using single letters

1. Ask your Learner to read the **sounds** of the letters at the top of the Learner page:
   r, t, m, u, p, g and *a*.
   • Explain to your Learner that they will use these letters to make words.

2. Show how to use the sounds to build the word **rat** by sounding out the letters.
   • Sound out **rat** letter by letter, *r-a-t* and write it down.

3. Work with your Learner to build other two or three-letter words. (Four is fine too.)
   • Invite your Learner to write down the words or write the words for them.
   • Use letter cards (available from the Shannon Trust website), so that your Learner can move the letters around. This hands-on approach really helps learning.
   • Praise your Learner if they sound things out correctly, even if they make non-words. Discuss these with your Learner.
   • If you are working with an ESOL Learner you may need to tell them the words and ask them to find the letters.

Tip: There are over 20 two or three-letter words that can be made using these letters. Aim for at least ten. The same letter can be used twice in one word, such as **gag**.

Notes:

Word build
Make words using the letters

r t m u p g a

	r
	t
	m
	u
	p
	g
	a

Spot the words

Learners look for the Sight Words **I**, **the**, **to** and **was**

Your Learner **should not** attempt to sound out these Sight Words.

1. Read the words **I**, **the**, **to**, **was** to your Learner.
   • Explain to your Learner that there are some everyday words that they need to recognise without sounding them out. These are called **Sight Words**.
   • Point out that **I** on its own is always a capital letter.
   • Ask your Learner to read the words.

2. Ask your Learner to search the small boxes on the Learner page for the word **I**.
   • Tick the word every time they find it. (There are 2.) Write the number on the notepad.

3. Ask your Learner to search the small boxes for the word **the**.
   • Tick the word every time they find it. Write down on the notepad how many there are. (5)
   • Do the same for the words **to** (6) and **was** (3).

Tip: Show your Learner some everyday text such as in a newspaper and highlight the word **the** whenever it occurs.

Notes:

Spot the words
Find these everyday Sight Words

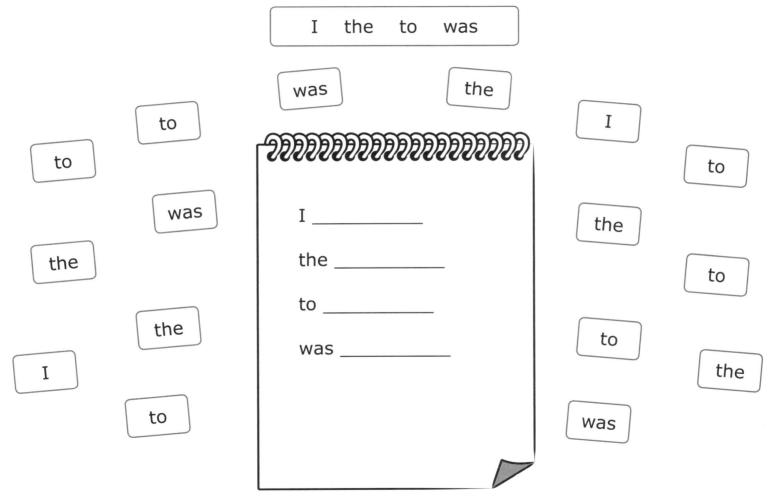

I   the   to   was

was   the

to   I

to   to

was   the

the   to

the   to

I

to   was

Text and check

Learners read short sentences that use everyday Sight Words

1. Ask your Learner to read the Sight Words **I**, **the**, **to** and **was** on the Learner page.
   Tell them that the other words in the sentences need to be sounded out.

2. Ask your Learner to read the sentences and tick all the sentences they get right.
   - Encourage your Learner to do the ticks.
   - Tell your Learner that all sentences start with a **capital letter** and finish with a **full stop**.
   - Point out the words with capital letters: **I**, **It** and remind them they have the same sound as lower case letters.
   - Underline any errors.

3. Make a note in the Notes box of any words that are underlined.
   - Go over these words again once or twice and then ask your Learner to read the sentence again.
   - If any words remain a problem, or take two or three times to get right, add them to the Parking page (page 65).

Tip: Go over problem words again in the next session before moving on. Look again at the alphabet chart on page 25 if your Learner struggles to recognise the capital letters.

Notes:

| I | the | to | was |

	✓
I ran a shop.	
It had to shut.	
I was sad to shut the shop.	
It was the best job I had.	

Spot the words

Learners look for the Sight Words **he, she, me, we** and **be**

Your Learner **should not** attempt to sound out these Sight Words.

1. Remind your Learner that these are everyday words they need to recognise without sounding them out.
   - Point out that some are the same words but with a capital letter as they are often found at the beginning of a sentence.

2. Read the words **he, she, me, we, be** on the Learner page.
   - Point out that they all have the same ending (e).
   - Ask your Learner to read the words.

3. Show your Learner how to search the small boxes for the word **he**.
   - Tick the word every time you find it (there are 4). Write the number on the notepad.

4. Ask your Learner to search the small boxes for the word **she**.
   - Tick the word every time they find it. Write down on the notepad how many there are. (3)
   - Do the same for the other words: **me** (2), **we** (3), **be** (4).

Tip: Support your Learner to count and write down numbers if they have difficulty with this.

Notes:

Spot the words
Find these everyday Sight Words

he   she   me   we   be

he   She

he   be

we   me

she   he

He   We

we   she

me   be

be   be

he _____

she _____

me _____

we _____

be _____

Read and check

Learners read the Sight Words **he**, **she**, **me**, **we**, **be**, **I**, **the**, **was** and **to**

1. Remind your Learner that the words in the grid opposite are Sight Words. They must not try to sound them out.
   • Point out that some of the words have capital letters.

2. Ask your Learner to read each word in the grid on the Learner page.
   • Tick all the words they get right and leave the others blank.
   • Read to your Learner any words that have not been ticked. Ask your Learner to read them again.

3. When your Learner has finished, go over any words that have not been ticked:
   • Read them to your Learner (do not sound them out).
   • Ask your Learner to read them again and tick the ones they get right.

4. If any words remain a problem or take two or three tries to get right, write them in the Notes box and do 'Look and Say, Copy and Say' (as you do on the Parking page on page 65) until your Learner is confident.

Tip: Point out that **I** on its own always has a capital letter.

Notes:

Read and check
Read these everyday Sight Words

	✓
he	
the	
we	
I	
she	
be	
was	
to	
the	
was	

	✓
He	
She	
We	
The	
Be	
The	
He	
to	
was	
be	

	✓
she	
the	
I	
me	
he	
to	
we	
was	
me	
be	

Text and check

Learners read simple sentences that use the Sight Words **he**, **she**, **me**, **we**, **be**, **I**, **the**, **to** and **was**

1. Ask your Learner to read the Sight Words **he**, **she**, **me**, **we**, **be**, **I**, **the, to** and **was** on the Learner page.

2. Ask your Learner to read the sentences in the grid.
   - Tick all the ones they get right and leave the others blank.

3. Go over any sentences that have not been ticked.
   - Underline any errors in each sentence.
   - Read them to your Learner.
   - Ask your Learner to read the sentences again and to tick the ones they get right.

4. Make a note of any words that are a problem in the Notes box. Go over these once or twice.
   - If your Learner has difficulty recognising capital letters, look again at page 29.

5. If any words remain a problem, or take two or three tries to get right, add them to the Parking page (page 65).

Tip: Ask some questions about the sentences to check understanding, such as: What time can they meet at the pub?

Notes:

| he   she   me   we   be   I   the   to   was |

	✓
I wish she was not with me.	
We can be at the pub at ten.	
He was sad and fed up.	
Max had a chat with me.	
The van hit the lad.	
We had to lock up the shed.	
She had jet lag.	
The thin cat got the fat rat.	
The fox bit the hen.	
The bag had a big zip.	
The cup had a chip in it.	
I am not fit to jog yet.	

Use the page opposite to note down any sounds or words you have come across so far in the manual that your Learner needs to practise again. Do this activity when you have completed all the other activities.

1. Write the words in the first (Park) column as you come across them in the manual.

2. When your Learner gets to this page:
   - Take **one** word at a time.
   - Read it to your Learner and sound it out. (Note: Sight Words are **not** sounded out.)
   - Remind them that some sounds are made from more than one letter such as th, sh, ch and ck.
   - Ask your Learner to read the word.
   - Ask your Learner to copy and say it.
   - Tick it if it's right.
   - Repeat the whole process with the same word: Copy and Say, Copy and Say until they are confident with it. Repeat on a new row if needed.

3. Repeat the 'Look and Say, Copy and Say' process with all the other words in the Park column.
   - If your Learner continues to struggle with a word, make sure they know what the word means and try putting it into sentences for them.

Tip: Use the alphabet charts to help if your Learner needs it.

Notes:

Parking page

Park. Look and Say	✓

Copy and Say	✓

Copy and Say	✓

Copy and Say	✓

Parking page

Use the page opposite to note down any more words your Learner needs to practise again. Treat in the same way as outlined on the previous Parking page.

Tip:

Notes:

Park. Look and Say	✓

Copy and Say	✓

Copy and Say	✓

Copy and Say	✓

Progress check

Explain to your Learner that this is a good point in Turning Pages to see how things are going and that they are confident with what they have learned so far.

Ask your Learner to read each letter sound in this part of the Progress check.
- Tick everything they get right and leave the others blank.
- Use the Turning Pages Reading Level to show your Learner how much they have achieved.
- Keep a note of any letter sounds they are not confident with. Your Learner can practise them at the beginning of the next session.

Turning Pages Reading Levels

All or most of the letters sounded out correctly. (No more than 10 errors.)	TP Level 1.0

Explain to your Learner that the levels given are only relevant to Turning Pages. They give a clear picture of their progress in the reading programme and their achievements so far.

Tip:

Notes:

Read and tick all the letter sounds you know

	✓
a	
k	
p	
w	
b	
i	
h	
m	
j	
o	
t	
qu	
u	
r	
g	

	✓
x	
e	
l	
n	
d	
v	
z	
y	
s	
c	
f	
ck	
sh	
ch	
th	

	✓
M	
D	
A	
G	
P	
N	
O	
B	
K	
R	
Qu	
T	
V	
Y	

	✓
U	
C	
F	
J	
L	
E	
W	
H	
I	
X	
Z	
S	

TP Level 1.0 [ ]

Turning Pages Reading Levels

1. Ask your Learner to read each word and sentence in this part of the Progress check.

2. Tick everything they get right and leave the others blank.

All or most of the short words read correctly. (No more than 5 errors.)	**TP Level 1.1**
All or most of the words in the sentences read correctly. (No more than 5 errors.)	**TP Level 1.2**

If your Learner makes more than 10 errors overall you will need to go over the relevant activities again and spend some more time practising with the Turning Pages reading books. When you have done this, try the Progress check again.

If your Learner continues to have problems, they may need specialist help.

Tip:

Notes:

Read and tick all the words you know

	✓
web	
dog	
fun	
ram	
zip	
pub	

	✓
beg	
chin	
can	
quit	
log	
rush	

	✓
jam	
box	
moth	
yes	
kit	
suck	

	✓
cat	
fit	
hid	
shed	
much	
thin	

TP Level 1.1

Read these sentences

	✓
The cat ran in with a big fish.	
She sat on the bed to chat to me.	
He got a bug and was sick.	

TP Level 1.2

71

The Turning Pages Reading Levels show your Learner what they have achieved.

Congratulate them and explain what each level means (as outlined on the previous Mentor pages).

Ask your Learner if there any letters or words that they would like to go over again. Make a note of them below.

Go over them before moving on.

 Your Learner has achieved the skills to read the dark blue Turning Pages reading books coded Level 1.2

Tip:

Notes:

Congratulations!

You are now reading single letters, blending sounds together and reading some Sight Words and short sentences.

You are now reading at **TP Level 1.2**.

Next we are going to look at:
- Double letters
- The plural s
- Four and five-letter words
- More Sight Words

Listen and count

Learners identify the number of sounds in words

Words to read

1. tell   *t-e-ll* (3)
2. stiff   *s-t-i-ff* (4)
3. mess   *m-e-ss* (3)
4. egg   *e-gg* (2)
5. fizz   *f-i-zz* (3)
6. toss   *t-o-ss* (3)
7. add   *a-dd* (2)
8. still   *s-t-i-ll* (4)

Tip: It may help to tap out the sounds: one tap for each sound.

This task is not about spelling so it is best that you do the writing for your Learner.

1. Tell your Learner that they are going to listen for letter sounds. Read out the first word **tell** from the Words to read box. Sound it out: ***t-e-ll*** (3 sounds).
   - On the Learner page circle the number of **sounds** in the word tell (3 sounds).
   - Write **tell** and sound it out, pointing to the letters or letter combinations, that make each sound.
   - Point out the double letters (**ll**) and explain that double letters at the end of a word make just one sound.

2. Read the second word **stiff** to your Learner and sound it out: ***s-t-i-ff***
   - Ask your Learner to circle the number of **sounds** they can hear in the word (4 sounds).
   - Write the word for your Learner and sound it out again.
   - Point out the double letters that make one sound.

3. Do the same with each of the other words.

Notes:

Listen and count

Count the number of sounds you can hear in each word

	The number of sounds				The whole word
1.	1	2	③	4	_____
2.	1	2	3	4	_____
3.	1	2	3	4	_____
4.	1	2	3	4	_____
5.	1	2	3	4	_____
6.	1	2	3	4	_____
7.	1	2	3	4	_____
8.	1	2	3	4	_____

Read and check

Learners read three and four-letter words including some with double letters

1. Remind your Learner that sometimes more than one letter is used to represent one sound.
   - Use the alphabet chart to point out **sh**, **ch** and **th**.
   - Remind them about **ck** that comes at the end of words and has the sound *c*.
   - Remind your Learner that double letters at the end of words also make just one sound.

2. When your Learner has finished, go over any words that have not been ticked.
   - Read each of these words and sound them out and read again.
   - Ask your Learner to read them again and tick the ones they get right.

3. Make a note of any words that are still a problem in the Notes box.
   - Go over these words again once or twice.
   - If any words remain a problem, or take two or three tries to get right, add them to the blank column on page 81. Your Learner can practise them again when you reach that page.

Tip: Use the alphabet charts to support your Learner if needed.

Notes:

Read and check
Check that you can read short words

	✓
sun	
buzz	
hit	
hill	
mess	
pip	
egg	
shut	
fizz	
much	
jug	
sick	
leg	
miss	
add	
with	
bell	

	✓
wet	
toss	
such	
van	
fizz	
fuss	
stop	
bob	
will	
sell	
thin	
well	
hut	
rag	
boss	
tax	
tell	

Listen and point

Learners match sounds to letters including those with a plural s

Words to read

1. tins   *t-i-n-s*
2. at   *a–t*
3. pins   *p-i-n-s*
4. pat   *p-a-t*
5. an   *a–n*
6. taps   *t-a-p-s*
7. in   *i–n*
8. dots   *d-o-t-s*

Tip: Point out that the **s** in some words can sound more like a **z** such as: ***p-i-n-s***.

1. Ask your Learner to read the sounds at the top of the Learner page:
   s, a, i, p, t, n, d, o
   • Explain that you are going to put these sounds together to make words and that some words will have an **s** sound on the end.
   • The letter s on the end of a word can mean more than one item (plural), such as one cat, lots of cats.
   • Emphasise the last sound as Learners often hear the first sound in a word but not the last one.

2. Tell your Learner to listen to the sounds.
   • Read out the first word: **tins**
   • Sound it out pointing to each letter as you go : *t-i-n-s*
   • Read the word again showing how the letters blend.
   • Write the letters in the boxes and the word **tins** on the line.

3. Read the second word and sound it out: **at/*a-t***
   • Ask your Learner to point to each letter as you say the sound.
   • Invite them to write the letters in and to say the word.

4. Do the same for each of the other words.

Notes:

Listen and point
Match the sounds you hear to the letters you see

| s a i p t n d o |

1. ☐☐☐☐   = _____

2. ☐☐   = _____

3. ☐☐☐☐   = _____

4. ☐☐☐   = _____

5. ☐☐   = _____

6. ☐☐☐☐   = _____

7. ☐☐   = _____

8. ☐☐☐☐   = _____

Read and check

Learners read three and four-letter words including those with a plural s

1. Ask your Learner to read each word in the grid on the Learner page.
   • Tick all the words they get right and leave the others blank.

2. When your Learner has finished, go over any words that have not been ticked.
   • Read each of these words and sound them out and read again.
   • Ask your Learner to read them again and tick the ones they get right.

3. Make a note of any words that are still a problem in the Notes box.
   • Go over these words again once or twice.
   • If any words remain a problem, or take two or three tries to get right, add them to the blank column on page 93. Your Learner can practise them again when you reach that page.

Tip: Use the alphabet charts to support your Learner if needed.

Notes:

Read and check

Check that you can read short words

	✓
dens	
taps	
in	
nets	
at	
pop	
bags	
hit	
fin	
can	
jugs	
kit	
legs	
man	
got	
on	
ribs	

	✓
sun	
dig	
tug	
vans	
win	
zips	
tax	
bob	
wet	
it	
guns	
pets	
hut	
rob	
red	
up	
hens	

Words from page 77	✓

Gap fill
Learners read short sentences and fill in the missing words

1. Explain to your Learner that they will read some sentences that have one word missing.
   - They will choose the right word from the words in brackets to complete the sentence.
   - They should read the sentence more than once to make sure of the meaning.

2. Read out the first sentence on the Learner page: **He had six _____.** and then read the words in the next column **dog, dogs**.
   - Show your Learner how to complete the sentence by trying each word from the brackets.
   - Write in the correct word: **dogs**.
   - Read the complete sentence again to help your Learner make sense of it.

3. Support your Learner to do the same with the other sentences.
   - Read it with them if needed.
   - Each time ask your Learner to try both words to see which one makes sense.

Tip: Support your Learner if English is not their first language. Read out the sentences and ask which one makes sense. Talk about other objects around you that can have a plural **s**.

Notes:

Gap fill
Complete these sentences so that they make sense

1.	He had six _____.	dog, dogs
2.	She sat up in _____.	beds, bed
3.	Sam had red _____ .	socks, sock
4.	The bin had ten _____ in it.	can, cans
5.	The man ran to get on the _____.	ship, ships
6.	The lad got off the bus with a bag of _____.	chips, chip
7.	The duck sat on the six _____ in the nest.	eggs, egg
8.	She had a sick _____.	cats, cat
9.	He got me a _____.	hat, hats

Spot the word

Learners look for the Sight Words **what**, **have**, **you**, **for** and **of**

1. Read the words **what**, **have**, **you**, **for** and **of** on the Learner page to your Learner.
   • Explain that these are everyday Sight Words that they need to recognise without sounding them out.
   • Ask your Learner to read the words.

2. Ask your Learner to look at the words in the small boxes on the Learner page and find the word **what**.
   • Tick the word every time they find it. (There are 3.) Write the number on the notepad.

3. Now ask your Learner to search the small boxes on the page for each of the other words: **have** (4), **you** (3), **for** (3), **of** (2).
   • Tick the word when they find it and write the number on the notepad.

4. Support your Learner to read the sentence at the bottom of the page.
   • Ask them which of the 5 words at the top is NOT used in this sentence (**of**).
   • Point out the question mark and explain that this goes at the end of a sentence to show it is a question.

Tip: Show your Learner some everyday text, such as in a newspaper, and try to spot these everyday words wherever they appear.

Notes:

Spot the word
Find these everyday Sight Words

what   have   you   for   of

have

for

what

you

you

what

have

for

for

have

you

what

have

of

of

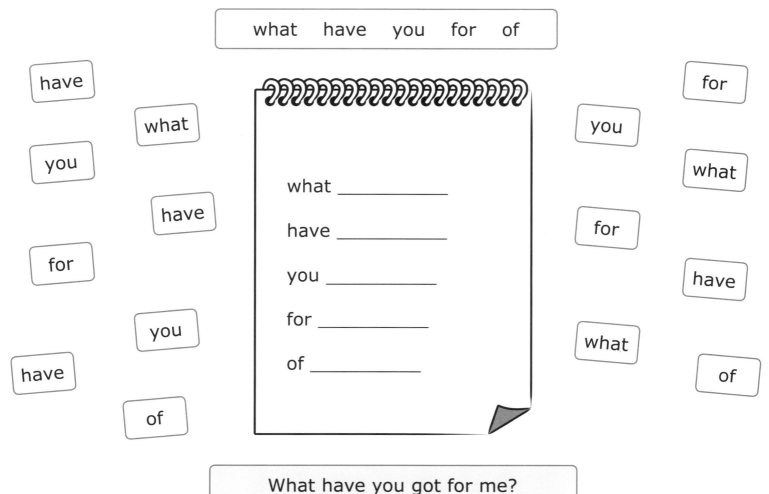

what _____

have _____

you _____

for _____

of _____

What have you got for me?

85

Read and check

Learners practise reading Sight Words

1. Remind your Learner that these are Sight Words on the Learner page. They must not try to sound them out.
   • Point out that some of the words have a capital letter.

2. Ask your Learner to read each word in the grid.
   • Tell them to tick all the words they get right and leave the others blank.

3. When your Learner has finished, go over any words that have not been ticked:
   • Read them to your Learner (do not sound them out).
   • Ask your Learner to read them again and tick the ones they get right.

4. If any words remain a problem or take two or three tries to get right, write them in the Notes box and do 'Look and Say, Copy and Say' (as you do on the Parking page) until your Learner is confident.

Tip: Encourage your Learner to see these words as a whole but tell them that the first letter sound can be a clue to reading the word.

Notes:

Read and check
Check that you can read these Sight Words

	✓
what	
have	
you	
for	
of	
The	
I	
to	
was	
he	
She	
me	
be	
he	
the	
You	
me	

	✓
for	
be	
have	
of	
to	
we	
What	
I	
she	
you	
of	
was	
Have	
for	
was	
the	
what	

Text and check

Learners read sentences with some Sight Words

1. Ask your Learner to read the Sight Words **what**, **have**, **you**, **for** and **of** on the Learner page.
   - If you need to, practise the words with your Learner.

2. Ask your Learner to read the sentences in the grid.
   - Tick all the ones they get right and leave the others blank.

3. Go over any sentences that have not been ticked.
   - Underline any errors in each sentence.
   - Read them to your Learner.
   - Ask your Learner to read the sentences again and to tick the ones they get right.

4. Make a note of any words that are a problem in the Notes box. Go over these once or twice.

5. If any words remain a problem, or take two or three tries to get right, add them to the Parking page (page 109).

Tip: Ask your Learner some questions about the sentences to check their understanding, such as: What was in the pot? or Who will have a chat?

Notes:

Text and check
Read these sentences that have some Sight Words

| what | have | you | for | of |

	✓
I have a bag of chips.	
What is that for?	
You and Ben can have a chat.	
I have a pot of jam.	
He was sick of his job.	
What can I get for him?	
You have got a lot of cash.	
You have lots of luck.	
This is for you.	
What is this big box for?	

Listen

Learners listen and identify the order of sounds in spoken words

Words to read

1. trap   *t-r-a-p*
2. slip   *s-l-i-p*
3. step   *s-t-e-p*
4. slot   *s-l-o-t*
5. grub   *g-r-u-b*
6. club   *c-l-u-b*
7. pram   *p-r-a-m*
8. trim   *t-r-i-m*

Tip: It may be tricky for your Learner to hear the **second letter sound**. If so try saying the word without the first letter, such as in the word trap. Say **rap** first and then put the *t* in front: **trap**

You may need to sound out the words more than once so that your Learner can hear the order of sounds.

1. Read out the first word: **trap**
- Sound out the word clearly: *t-r-a-p*
- Ask your Learner:
  - What is the first sound you can hear? *t*
  - What is the second sound? *r*
  - What is the next sound? *a*
  - What is the last sound you can hear? *p*
- Write the separate letters in the spaces on the Learner page.
- Say the whole word again blending the sounds. Write the whole word.

2. Repeat the steps above for each word in the Words to read box.
- Ask your Learner to listen and identify each sound in the words.
- Use the alphabet on the Learner page to find the correct letters for each sound.
- Ask your Learner to write the letters in the spaces and then to write the whole word.
- Explain to your Learner that they do not need to worry about handwriting.
- Emphasise the *o* and *u* vowel sounds as they can be easily confused.

Notes:

Listen

Listen for the different sounds in each word

a b c d e f g h i j k l m n o p qu r s t u v w x y z

1. ☐ ☐ ☐ ☐   = _____

2. ☐ ☐ ☐ ☐   = _____

3. ☐ ☐ ☐ ☐   = _____

4. ☐ ☐ ☐ ☐   = _____

5. ☐ ☐ ☐ ☐   = _____

6. ☐ ☐ ☐ ☐   = _____

7. ☐ ☐ ☐ ☐   = _____

8. ☐ ☐ ☐ ☐   = _____

Read and check

Learners read four and five-letter words

1. Ask your Learner to read each word in the grid on the Learner page.
   • Tick all the words they get right. Leave the others blank.

2. When your Learner has finished, go over any words that have not been ticked.
   • Read each of these words and sound them out and read again.
   • Ask your Learner to read them again and tick the ones they get right.

3. Make a note of any words that are still a problem in the Notes box.
   • Go over these words again once or twice.
   • If any words remain a problem, or take two or three tries to get right, add them to the blank column on page 97. Your Learner can practise them again when you reach that page.

Tip: Use the alphabet charts to support your Learner if needed.

Notes:

Read and check
Check that you can read these short words

	✓
slim	
trip	
crabs	
flap	
slit	
prop	
brag	
steps	
from	
clan	
snuff	
brim	
skim	
drab	
flab	
plot	
crib	

	✓
stun	
drag	
slug	
swam	
swim	
drugs	
slum	
still	
glass	
plan	
snag	
gram	
stub	
plop	
flag	
slam	
plums	

Words from page 81	✓

Gap fill
Learners complete four-letter words with the second letter missing

Words to find
1. step
2. slit, spit,
3. drab, stab, crab, grab
4. glum, plum, drum
5. blot, slot, spot, plot
6. from

Tip: Use individual letter cards so that your Learner can move the letters around.

1. Ask your Learner to read the sounds at the top of the Learner page: **r**, **t**, **l** and **p**

2. Ask your Learner to look at the first incomplete word on the list: **s _ ep**
   - Show that by trying out all the letters you can make the word **step**. Try all the letters but explain that srep, slep or spep are not real words.
   - Write in the missing letter **t**.

3. Ask your Learner to do the same with the other words using each letter in turn.
   - Make sure your Learner does not miss out or misread the second letter in a word as the meaning of the word can be affected.

4. Discuss any non-words that they may come up with. Praise their phonic skills but make sure they only write in the real words.
   - Explain that the number of gapped words on the page shows how many real words can be made.

Notes:

Gap fill
Use letters to complete words

```
r   t   l   p
```

1.	s __ ep			
2.	s __ it	s __ it		
3.	d __ ab	s __ ab	c __ ab	g __ ab
4.	g __ um	p __ um	d __ um	
5.	b __ ot	s __ ot	s __ ot	p __ ot
6.	f __ om			

Read and check

Learners read four and five-letter words

1. Ask your Learner to read each word in the grid on the Learner page.
  • Tick all the words they get right and leave the others blank.

2. When your Learner has finished, go over any words that have not been ticked.
  • Read each of these words and sound them out and read again.
  • Ask your Learner to read them again and tick the ones they get right.

3. Make a note of any words that are still a problem in the Notes box.
  • Go over these words again once or twice.
  • If any words remain a problem, or take two or three tries to get right, add them to the blank column on page 101. Your Learner can practise them again when you reach that page.

Tip: Use the alphabet charts to support your Learner if needed.

Notes:

	✓
spin	
trap	
trim	
stem	
slat	
still	
brim	
swell	
from	
crabs	
slug	
swill	
plug	
snap	
glum	
plop	
crib	

	✓
dress	
swig	
cliffs	
swam	
twins	
flip	
pram	
flop	
smell	
slit	
grin	
spit	
plums	
stiff	
drug	
brag	
stem	

Words from page 93	✓

97

Word build

Learners make three and four-letter words using single letters

1. Ask your Learner to read the **sounds** of the letters at the top of the Learner page:
t, r, s, l, m, i, p, o and **a**
- Explain to your Learner that they will use these letters to make words.

2. Show how to use the letters to build the word **tram** by sounding out the letters.
- Sound out *t-r-a-m* letter by letter and write it down.

3. Work with your Learner to make other 3 or 4 letter words. Aim for at least 10.
- Ask your Learner to write down the words or write the words for them.
- It may help your Learner to use letter cards so that they can move the letters around.
- Praise your Learner when they sound things out correctly, even if they make non-words or shorter words. Discuss these with your Learner.
- Give extra support to Learners whose first language is not English by giving them the words and asking them to find the letters.

Tip: Over 20 four or five-letter words can be made using these letters. The same letter can be used twice in each word, such as **pill**, or an **s** can be added to make plurals.

Notes:

Word build
Make words using the letters

t r s l m i p o a

t

r

s

l

m

i

p

o

a

Read and check

Learners read four and five-letter words

1. Remind your Learner that when they see **double letters** on the end of a word it represents just **one sound**.

2. Ask your Learner to read each word in the grid.
   • Tick all the words they get right. Leave the others blank.

3. When your Learner has finished, go over any words that have not been ticked.
   • Read each of these words and sound them out.
   • Ask your Learner to read them again and tick the ones they get right.

4. Make a note of any words that are still a problem in the Notes box.
   • Go over these words again once or twice.
   • If any words remain a problem, or take two or three tries to get right, add them to the Parking page (page 109).

Tip: Use the alphabet charts to support your Learner if needed.

Notes:

Read and check
Check that you can read these words

	✓
spin	
traps	
trim	
stem	
slat	
still	
brim	
swell	
from	
crab	
slug	
swill	
plug	
snap	
grub	
plop	
cribs	

	✓
dress	
swig	
cliff	
swam	
twin	
flip	
pram	
flop	
smell	
slit	
grin	
spit	
plum	
stiff	
drugs	
brag	
slim	

Words from page 97	✓

Spot the word

Learners look for the Sight Words: **do, are, my, time, out** and **about**

1. Read the words **do**, **are**, **my**, **time**, **out** and **about** on the Learner page to your Learner.
   - Tell your Learner that these are Sight Words that are not sounded out.
   - Ask your Learner to read the words.

2. Show your Learner how to search the small boxes on the Learner page for the word **do**.
   (Tell them that it is a very short word.)
   - Tick the word **do** every time you find it (there are 3). Write how many times you find the word on the notepad.

3. Ask your Learner to look at the words in the small boxes on the Learner page and find the word **are**.
   - Tell your Learner to tick the word every time they find it and write down how many there are. (3)
   - Now ask your Learner to search the boxes for the word **my**. Tick the word every time they find it and write the number down. (There are 3.)
   - Do the same for the words **time**, **out** and **about**. (There are 2 of each word.)

Tip: The words **out** and **about** have the same ending. Point this out to your Learner.

Notes:

Spot the words
Find these everyday Sight Words

do are my time out about

about   do   are

are

out

my

time

my

do

my

do _____

are _____

my _____

time _____

out _____

about _____

about

do

time

are

out

103

Read and check

Learners practise reading Sight Words they have learned so far

1. Tell your Learner that they are going to practise reading the Sight Words they have learned so far.
   • Point out some of the words have a capital letter.

2. Remind your Learner that the Sight Words need to be remembered as whole words not sounded out.

3. Ask your Learner to read each word in the grid.
   • Tell them to tick all the words they get right and leave the others blank.

4. When your Learner has finished, go over any words that have not been ticked.
   • Read them to your Learner (do not sound them out).
   • Ask your Learner to read them again and tick the ones they get right.

5. If any words remain a problem, or take two or three tries to get right, write them in the Notes box and do 'Look and Say, Copy and Say' (as you do on the Parking page) until your Learner is confident.

Tip: Use your finger to uncover one word at a time. This will help your Learner to focus on each word.

Notes:

Read and check

Check that you can read these Sight Words

	✓
do	
are	
time	
my	
out	
about	
what	
have	
you	
For	
of	
he	
The	
to	
she	
I	
me	
was	

	✓
be	
do	
We	
are	
what	
time	
about	
have	
my	
was	
out	
you	
He	
for	
She	
of	
me	
do	

	✓
be	
Are	
we	
out	
the	
about	
to	
My	
I	
was	
Do	
my	
about	
time	
out	
are	
have	
the	

Text and check

Learners read sentences with Sight Words learned so far

1. Ask your Learner to read the Sight Words **do, are, my, time, out** and **about** on the Learner page.
   • If you need to, practise the words with your Learner.

2. Ask your Learner to read the sentences on the Learner page.
   • Tick the sentences they get right. Leave the others blank.
   • Remind your Learner that sentences start with a capital letter and finish with a full stop.
   • Point out that some of these are questions. They end with a question mark.

3. Go over any sentences that have not been ticked and underline any errors.
   • Read them to your Learner.
   • Ask your Learner to read the sentences again and to tick the ones they get right.

4. Make a note of any words that are a problem in the Notes box. Go over these once or twice.

5. If any words remain a problem, or take two or three tries to get right, add them to the Parking page (page 109).

Tip: Ask your Learner some questions about the sentences to check their understanding, such as: Who was stuck in the mud? and Who would not let the dog out?

Notes:

Text and check
Read these sentences with Sight Words you have learned so far

| do | are | my | time | out | about |

	✓
I have lots of jobs to do.	
Are you out of time for this job?	
My mum did not let the dog out.	
What time do I have to get up?	
Tell me what the film is about.	
You are just in time for the bus.	
Do you get out and about much?	
I get in my truck.	
The block was about to crush my leg.	
It is time to have a rest.	
The men are stuck in the mud.	
Do you have time for a snack?	

Use the page opposite to note down any sounds or words you have come across so far in the manual that your Learner needs to practise again. Do this activity when you have completed all the other activities.

1. Write the words in the first (Park) column as you come across them in the manual.

2. When your Learner gets to this page:
- Take **one** word at a time.
- Read it to your Learner and sound it out. (Note: Sight Words are **not** sounded out.)
- Ask your Learner to read the word.
- Ask your Learner to copy and say it.
- Tick it if it's right.
- Repeat the process with the same word: Copy and Say, Copy and Say until they are confident with it. Repeat on a new row if needed.

3. Repeat the 'Look and Say, Copy and Say' process with all the other words in the Park column.
- If your Learner continues to struggle with a word, make sure they know what the word means and try putting it into sentences for them.

Tip: Use the alphabet charts to help if your Learner needs it.

Notes:

Park. Look and Say	✓	Copy and Say	✓	Copy and Say	✓	Copy and Say	✓

Parking page

Use the page opposite to note down any more words your Learner needs to practise again. Treat in the same way as outlined on the previous Parking page.

Tip:

Notes:

Park. Look and Say	✓	Copy and Say	✓	Copy and Say	✓	Copy and Say	✓

Progress check

Explain to your Learner that this is a good point in Turning Pages to see how things are going and that they are confident with what they have learned so far.

Ask your Learner to read each word in the Progress check.
- Tick everything they get right.
- Leave blank any words that your Learner cannot read.
- Use the Turning Pages Reading Levels to show your Learner how much they have achieved.
- Keep a note of any words or letter sounds they are not confident with. Your Learner can practise them at the beginning of the next session.

Turning Pages Reading Levels

All or most of the words sounded out correctly including double letters and plurals. (No more than 10 errors.)	**TP Level 1.3**
All or most of the short words read correctly. (No more than 5 errors.)	**TP Level 1.4**

Tip:

Notes:

Read and tick all the words you know

	✓
fill	
well	
mess	
fuss	
buzz	
add	
miss	
loss	
hiss	
cull	
puff	
sell	
mill	

	✓
tins	
hats	
dogs	
ships	
zips	
cups	
eggs	
fans	
socks	
pens	
tubs	
chops	
kids	

	✓
stop	
clap	
grim	
frog	
plan	
snap	
stem	
grub	
flag	
prod	
grab	
spell	
trip	

	✓
grill	
slim	
club	
press	
slip	
snag	
flesh	
gruff	
press	
brim	
snack	
brick	
crab	

TP Level 1.3 ☐

TP Level 1.4 ☐

Turning Pages Reading Levels

1. Ask your Learner to read each word and sentence in this part of the Progress check.

2. Tick everything they get right and leave the others blank.

All or most of the Sight Words read correctly. (No more than 5 errors.)	**TP Level 1.5**
All or most of the words in the sentences read correctly. (No more than 5 errors.)	**TP Level 1.6**

If your Learner makes more than 10 errors overall (in both words and sentences) you will need to go over the relevant activities again and spend some more time practising with the Turning Pages reading books. When you have done this, try the Progress check again.

If your Learner continues to have problems they may need specialist help.

Tip:

Notes:

Read and tick all the Sight Words you know

	✓
he	
she	
me	
be	
we	
the	
to	

	✓
I	
was	
what	
have	
you	
for	
of	

	✓
do	
time	
are	
out	
about	
my	

TP Level 1.5

Read these sentences

	✓
Sam will do up the van for my dad.	
The lads had a lot of time to get to the club.	
The ship was out and about in the docks.	
What have you got in the sacks?	
She was about to slip on the wet grass.	

TP Level 1.6

115

The Turning Pages Reading Levels show your Learner what they have achieved.

Congratulate them and explain what each level means.

Ask your Learner if there any letters or words that they would like to go over again. Make a note of them below.

Go over them before moving on.

 Your Learner has achieved the skills to read the dark blue Turning Pages reading books coded Level 1.6

Tip:

Notes:

Congratulations!

You are reading words with double letters, the plural s, more Sight Words and short sentences with longer words in them.

You are now reading at **TP Level 1.6**.

Next we are going to look at:
- More four and five-letter words
- More Sight Words
- Breaking longer words down into syllables

Listen and count

Learners identify the number of sounds in words

Words to read

1. plan   *p-l-a-n* (4)
2. bat   *b-a-t* (3)
3. in   *i-n* (2)
4. crab   *c-r-a-b* (4)
5. thin   *th-i-n* (3)
6. drug   *d-r-u-g* (4)
7. mess   *m-e-ss* (3)
8. stop   *s-t-o-p* (4)
9. ships *sh-i-p-s* (4)

Tip: It may help your Learner to tap out the sounds: one tap for each sound.

This task is not about spelling so it is best if you do the writing for your Learner.

1. Ask your Learner to listen for the letter sounds in words.
- Read out the first word: **plan**. Then sound out the word: *p-l-a-n* (4 sounds).
- On the Learner page, circle the correct number to show the number of sounds.
- Write the word for your Learner and sound it out again pointing to the letters or letter combinations that make each sound.

2. Read the second word **bat** to your Learner and sound it out: *b-a-t*
- Ask your Learner to circle the number of **sounds** they can hear in the word. (3)
- Ask your Learner what sounds they heard. Write the word for your Learner and sound it out again.

3. Do the same for each of the other words.

Notes:

Listen and count

Count the number of sounds you can hear in each word

	The number of sounds				The whole word
1.	1	2	3	(4)	_____
2.	1	2	3	4	_____
3.	1	2	3	4	_____
4.	1	2	3	4	_____
5.	1	2	3	4	_____
6.	1	2	3	4	_____
7.	1	2	3	4	_____
8.	1	2	3	4	_____
9.	1	2	3	4	_____

Listen

Learners listen and identify the order of sounds in spoken words

Words to read

1. lamp   *l-a-m-p*
2. golf   *g-o-l-f*
3. lump   *l-u m-p*
4. lift   *l-i-f-t*
5. bent   *b-e-n-t*
6. best   *b-e-s-t*
7. tilt   *t-i-l-t*
8. tusk   *t-u-s-k*

Tip: Some Learners find it hard to hear the last sound in a word. The **last but one** sound can be even more difficult to hear. Point to the letters as you sound out the words.

1. Read out the first word: **lamp**
   - Sound out the word letter by letter: *l-a-m-p*
   - Ask your Learner:
     - What is the first sound you can hear? *l*
     - What is the second sound? *a*
     - What is the next sound? *m*
     - What is the last sound you can hear? *p*
   - Write the separate letters in the spaces on the Learner page.
   - Say the whole word again blending the sounds. Write the whole word.
   - You may need to sound out words more than once.

2. Repeat the steps above for each word in the Words to read box.
   - Ask your Learner to listen and identify each sound in the words.
   - Use the alphabet on the Learner page to find the correct letters for each sound.
   - Ask your Learner to write the letters in the spaces and then to write the whole word.
   - Explain to your Learner that they don't need to worry about their handwriting.

Notes:

a b c d e f g h i j k l m n o p qu r s t u v w x y z

1. l a m p   __**lamp**__

2. __ __ __ __   _____

3. __ __ __ __   _____

4. __ __ __ __   _____

5. __ __ __ __   _____

6. __ __ __ __   _____

7. __ __ __ __   _____

8. __ __ __ __   _____

Read and check
Learners read four and five-letter words

Listen carefully to check that your Learner is sounding out **each** letter correctly before blending the sounds into the word.

1. Ask your Learner to read each word in the grid on the Learner page, sounding it out letter by letter and then saying the whole word.
   - Tick all the words they get right. Leave the others blank.

2. When your Learner has finished, go over any words that have not been ticked.
   - Read each of these words and sound them out and read again.
   - Ask your Learner to read them again and tick the ones they get right.

3. Make a note of any words that are still a problem in the Notes box.
   - Go over these words again once or twice.
   - If any words remain a problem, or take two or three tries to get right, add them to the blank column on page 129. Your Learner can practise them again when you reach that page.

Tip: Tell your Learner that there are four or five sounds in every word, each one made by a single letter.

Notes:

	✓
soft	
test	
mash	
jump	
silt	
belt	
bumps	
sift	
felt	
camp	
pant	
help	
lump	
lost	
gust	
tilt	
maps	

	✓
daft	
tank	
bent	
rank	
tent	
fact	
milk	
films	
held	
left	
pump	
pest	
just	
sift	
golf	
melt	
lift	

Gap fill

Learners use letters to complete four-letter words with the last but one letter missing

Words to find

1. camp
2. silt, sift
3. tusk
4. past
5. lost, loft
6. help, hemp

Tip: Use letter cards if you have them. Point out that people say 'past' in different ways depending on where they are from but this is fine.

1. Ask your Learner to read the sounds at the top of the Learner page: **m**, **t**, **l**, **f** and **s**

2. Ask your Learner to look at the first incomplete word on the list: **ca_p**
   • Show that by trying out all the letters you can make the word **camp**. Make sure that you try **all** the letters, but explain that **catp**, **calp**, **cafp** and **casp** are not real words.
   • Write in the missing letter to make the word **camp**.

3. Ask your Learner to do the same with the other words using each letter in turn.
   • Encourage your Learner to write in the letters.

4. Discuss any non-words that your Learner may come up with. Praise their phonic skills but make sure they only complete real words.
   • The number of gapped words on the page shows how many real words can be made.

Notes:

m	t	l	f	s

1.	ca __ p	
2.	si __ t	si __ t
3.	tu __ k	
4.	pa __ t	
5.	lo __ t	lo __ t
6.	he __ p	he __ p

Listen and point

Learners use vowels to complete the words they hear

Words to read

1. much   *m-u-ch*
2. rash   *r-a-sh*
3. with   *w-i-th*
4. latch   *l-a-tch*
5. help   *h-e-l-p*
6. lost   *l-o-s-t*
7. fetch   *f-e-tch*
8. milk   *m-i-l-k*
9. such   *s-u-ch*

Tip: Your Learner may prefer you to write for them.

1. Ask your Learner to read the sounds at the top of the Learner page: **a**, **e**, **i**, **o** and **u**
   - Remind them that these letters are called **vowels**.
   - Explain to your Learner that they will be using these letters to complete words.

2. Read the first word: **much**
   - Point to the gapped word and explain you are going to look for the missing sound.
   - Sound out the word and show your Learner how to find the missing sound: **u**
   - Write the vowel sound in the box and the word **much** on the line. Read the word again.

3. Read the second word **rash** to your Learner and sound it out: *r-a-sh*
   - Ask your Learner to point to the missing letter and write it in the box.
   - Ask your Learner to write the word and to read it.
   - Do the same for the other words.
   - Point out the **tch** in the words **latch** and **fetch**. Tell your Learner that the sound it makes is **ch**.
   - This makes the word look longer but it is still has only 3 sounds.

Notes:

Listen and point

Use vowel sounds to complete words

$$\boxed{\text{a} \quad \text{e} \quad \text{i} \quad \text{o} \quad \text{u}}$$

1. [m] [ ] [ch] = _____

2. [r] [ ] [sh] = _____

3. [w] [ ] [th] = _____

4. [l] [ ] [tch] = _____

5. [h] [ ] [l] [p] = _____

6. [l] [ ] [s] [t] = _____

7. [f] [ ] [tch] = _____

8. [m] [ ] [l] [k] = _____

9. [s] [ ] [ch] = _____

Read and check

Learners read short words including those that end with **sh**, **ch**, **th**, **tch** and **ck**

1. Tell your Learner that they are going to read short words that practise the sounds they have learned so far.

2. Ask your Learner to read each word in the grid on the Learner page.
   • Tick all the words they get right. Leave the others blank.

3. When your Learner has finished, go over any words that have not been ticked.
   • Read each of these words and sound them out and read again.
   • Ask your Learner to read them again and tick the ones they get right.

4. Make a note of any words that are still a problem in the Notes box.
   • Go over these words again once or twice.
   • If any words remain a problem, or take two or three tries to get right, add them to the blank column on page 133. Your Learner can practise them again when you reach that page.

Tip: Use the alphabet charts to support your Learner if needed.

Notes:

Read and check
Check that you can read these words

	✓
pick	
tilt	
camp	
fetch	
much	
pack	
batch	
sift	
bust	
rash	
self	
silk	
fetch	
dock	
film	
rush	

	✓
witch	
ditch	
posh	
went	
sick	
with	
catch	
such	
mess	
pitch	
pant	
yelp	
quick	
pump	
felt	
match	

Words from page 123	✓

Listen

Learners listen for the end sounds **ng**, **nk** and **nd**

Words to read

List 1	List 2
bank	lend
sing	bang
tank	song
hand	thank
rung	thing
bond	chunk
wing	fond
long	send

Tip: Your Learner may like to write in the missing letters to complete the words in the grid.

1. Read the words in the top box on the Learner page to your Learner: sa**ng**, wi**nk** and be**nd** highlighting the end sounds **ng**, **nk**, **nd**.
   - Point out that the end sound **ng** is a sound that comes from the back of your throat. The **ng** is hardly heard at all in the spoken word.

2. Read the first word in List 1 of the Words to read box: **bank**
   - Point out that the word ends in the sound **k** and tick the correct box on the Learner page.
   - Read the word again.

3. Read the next word in List 1: **sing**
   - Ask your Learner to listen for the end sound and tick the correct box on the Learner page.
   - Ask your Learner to say the word.
   - Repeat the task for all the words in List 1 and List 2.

Notes:

| | sa**ng** | wi**nk** | be**nd** |

List 1	g	k	d
ban		✓	
sin			
tan			
han			
run			
bon			
win			
lon			

List 2	g	k	d
len			✓
ban			
son			
than			
thin			
chun			
fon			
sen			

Read and check

Learners read short one-syllable words with a focus on end sounds

1. Ask your Learner to read each word in the grid on the Learner page.
   • Tick all the words they get right. Leave the others blank.

2. When your Learner has finished, go over any words that have not been ticked.
   • Read each of these words and sound them out.
   • Ask your Learner to read them again and tick the ones they get right.

3. Make a note of any words that are still a problem in the Notes box.
   • Go over these words again once or twice.
   • If any words remain a problem, or take two or three tries to get right, add them to the Parking page (page 167).

Tip: Remember that the way your Learner will say some words, such as **path**, will depend on their accent. Any version is fine.

Notes:

	✓
will	
pitch	
sing	
catch	
song	
rock	
end	
notch	
much	
lost	
bank	
hand	
link	
belt	
tent	
ramps	

	✓
weld	
rang	
loft	
hiss	
path	
dust	
fetch	
mess	
films	
with	
milk	
back	
hutch	
rush	
rich	
fish	

Words from page 129	✓

Word build

Learners make short words using **sh** and **ch**

1. Ask your Learner to read the **sounds** of the letters at the top of the Learner page:
   t, i, p, s, a, sh and **ch**
   • Explain to your Learner that they will use these letters and letter combinations to make words.

2. Show your Learner how to use the sounds to make the word **past**.
   • Sound out **p-a-s-t** slowly and write it down on the Learner page.

3. Work with your Learner to make as many other words as they can.
   • Invite your Learner to write down the words or write the words for them.
   • Use letter cards so that your Learner can move the letters around.
   • Praise your Learner if they sound things out correctly even if they make non-words. Discuss these with your Learner.
   • If you are working with an ESOL Learner, you may need to tell them the word and ask them to find the letters.

Tip: There are over 20 words that can be made using these letters. Aim for at least 10.

Notes:

Make words using the letters and sounds

| t | i | p | s | a | sh | ch |

t

i

p

s

a

sh

ch

Read and check

Learners recap on the phonic skills learned so far

1. Remind your Learner that words can be sounded out letter by letter and that some sounds are made of more than one letter such as **sh**, **th**, **ch**, **ck**, **tch**, **ng** and double letters.
   • In this activity they will be using all these skills.

2. Ask your Learner to read each word in the grid on the Learner page.
   • Tick all the words they get right. Leave the others blank.

3. When your Learner has finished go over any words that have not been ticked.
   • Read each word, sound it out and then ask your Learner to read it again.

4. Make a note of any words that are still a problem in the Notes box.
   • Go over these words again once or twice.
   • If any words remain a problem, or take two or three tries to get right, add them to the Parking page (page 167).

Tip: Point out to your Learner the words **split** and **spilt**. These have the same letters and look similar so your Learner needs to sound the letters out carefully in order.

Notes:

Beginning sounds	✓
clap	
cram	
thin	
spot	
flip	
shed	
twin	
plum	
drug	
dress	
snip	
smell	
chop	
brat	

End sounds	✓
cash	
tuck	
mess	
patch	
sink	
sift	
rank	
such	
ring	
with	
lost	
felt	
land	
lunch	

Both	✓
slash	
drink	
clump	
trend	
cloth	
trust	
spilt	
clutch	
split	
thick	
chest	
bring	
swift	
shelf	

Text and check
Learners read short sentences

1. Tell your Learner that they are going to read sentences that use many of the skills they have learned so far including:
   - Sounding out single letters
   - Sounding out letter combinations
   - Reading everyday Sight Words.

2. Ask your Learner to read the sentences on the Learner page.
   - Encourage your Learner to tick the sentences they get correct.
   - Underline any errors in each sentence.
   - Read them to your Learner.
   - Ask your Learner to read the sentence again and tick the ones they get right.

3. Make a note of any words that are still a problem in the notes box. Go over these words once or twice.

4. If any words remain a problem or take two or three tries to get right, add them to the Parking page (page 167).

Tip: Ask some questions about the sentences to check understanding, such as: What was wrong with the truck? and What fell off with a crash?

Notes:

Text and check
Read these sentences

	✓
He split the logs.	
Thank you for the drinks.	
I can trust him with the cash box.	
The shelf fell off with a crash.	
The clutch in the truck smelt hot.	
She spilt the milk on the dress.	
It was such a long time to stand still.	
The fox left a bad smell.	
She sang a song for me.	
He got it off his chest.	

Spot the word

Learners look for the Sight Words **no, go**, **they, all**, **put** and **I'm**

1. Read the words **no, go, they, all, put** and **I'm** on the Learner page to your Learner.
   - Remind your Learner that these are Sight Words and therefore need to be read as whole words and not sounded out.
   - Ask your Learner to read the words.

2. Show your Learner how to search the small boxes on the Learner page for the word **no**.
   - Show how you can use the first letter and the length of the word to help. Tell them to look for a short word beginning with **n**.
   - Tick the word every time you find it. Write the number you have found on the notepad. (There are 4.)

3. Now ask your Learner to search the small boxes for the word **go**. Tell them it looks like **no** but starts with a **g**. Tick the word. (There are 3.) Write the number on the notepad.

4. Do the same for the other words. (There are 2 of each word.)

Tip: If your Learner asks about the apostrophe in **I'm** tell them not to worry about it now as it is covered in detail later on in Turning Pages.

Notes:

Spot the word
Read and match more everyday Sight Words

no   go   they   all   put   I'm

no

I'm

they

go

go

I'm

no

all

put

no

they

put

all

go

no

no _____

go _____

they _____

all _____

put _____

I'm _____

Read and check

Learners practise reading Sight Words

1. Tell your Learner that this is an opportunity for them to practise reading the Sight Words they have learned so far.
   - Remind them that they must not sound out the words, although the first letter sound can sometimes provide a clue for the whole word.
   - Point out that some of the words have a capital letter.

2. Ask your Learner to read each word in the grid on the Learner page.
   - Tick all the words they get right. Leave the others blank.

3. When your Learner has finished, go over any words that have not been ticked:
   - Read them to your Learner (do not sound them out).
   - Ask your Learner to read them again and tick the ones they get right.

4. If any words remain a problem or take two or three tries to get right, write them in the Notes box and do 'Look and Say, Copy and Say' (as you do on the Parking page) until your Learner is confident.

Tip:

Notes:

Read and check
Check that you can read these Sight Words

	✓
no	
go	
They	
all	
put	
I'm	
what	
me	
was	
The	
do	
time	
no	
they	
put	
about	
are	
for	

	✓
no	
go	
they	
all	
put	
I'm	
are	
We	
to	
My	
out	
of	
have	
He	
be	
She	
You	
I	

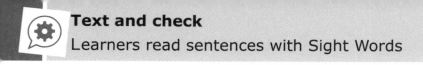

Text and check

Learners read sentences with Sight Words

1. Ask your Learner to read the Sight Words **no**, **go**, **they**, **all**, **put** and **I'm**.
   - If you need to, practise the words with your Learner.

2. Ask your Learner to read the sentences on the Learner page.
   - Tick the sentences they get right. Leave the others blank.
   - Remind your Learner once more that sentences start with a capital letter and finish with a full stop.
   - Point out that one of the sentences is a question and so it ends with a question mark.

3. Go over any sentences that have not been ticked.
   - Underline any errors in each sentence.
   - Read them to your Learner.
   - Ask your Learner to read the sentences again and to tick the ones they get right.

4. Make a note of any words that are a problem in the Notes box. Go over these once or twice.

5. If any words remain a problem, or take two or three tries to get right, add them to the Parking page (page 167).

Tip: Ask some questions about the sentences to check understanding, such as: What should go in the bin? and What do they hope to catch in the trap?

Notes:

no go they all put I'm

	✓
They put all the eggs in a box.	
Put all the scraps in the bin.	
They go out to the shops.	
I'm not fit for the trip with him.	
I put a trap in to catch the rats.	
I'm off for a trip out with all the lads.	
They have put all the bricks in that shed.	
The trams go to and from the docks.	
She had no cash left for lunch.	
We had no crab left to sell.	
Do you have time for a snack?	

Listen and count

Learners identify syllables in order to read longer words

Words to read

1. fan/tas/tic (3)
2. mag/net (2)
3. hand /bag (2)
4. pic/nic (2)
5. com/pu/ter (3)
6. sun/set (2)
7. lap/top (2)
8. in/for/ma/tion (4)
9. van (1)

Tip: Ask your Learner to put their hand under their chin as they say each word. Point out that they will feel their chin drop slightly when they say each syllable.

1. Tell your Learner that when reading longer words it helps to break them up into smaller chunks called **syllables**.

2. Ask your Learner to listen and watch as you say the first word: **fantastic**
   - Say the word again and tap out each chunk (syllable) on the table as you say it: **fan/tas/tic**
   - Circle the correct number of syllables on the Learner page (3 syllables).
   - Write the word and draw a line between each syllable as shown.

3. Read the second word: **magnet** and then say it again tapping out the syllables: **mag/net** (2 syllables).
   - Ask your Learner to repeat the word and then circle the number of syllables they can hear.
   - Write the word for your Learner and mark in the syllables with pencil lines.
   - Do the same with each of the other words.
   - Tell your Learner that every syllable has at least one vowel in it – **a**, **e**, **i**, **o** or **u**. Point this out using the first 2 words on the page.

4. Now ask your Learner to find the vowels in each syllable of each word and underline them.

Notes:

	The number of sounds				The whole word
1.	1	2	③	4	_____
2.	1	2	3	4	_____
3.	1	2	3	4	_____
4.	1	2	3	4	_____
5.	1	2	3	4	_____
6.	1	2	3	4	_____
7.	1	2	3	4	_____
8.	1	2	3	4	_____
9.	1	2	3	4	_____

Listen and point

Learners make two-syllable words

Read:

1. picnic	pic/nic
2. into	in/to
3. victim	vic/tim
4. upset	up/set
5. rucksack	ruck/sack
6. finish	fin/ish
7. kidnap	kid/nap
8. magnet	mag/net

Tip: Cross off each syllable when it has been matched. This will help your Learner see what there is left to do.
Highlighting the vowels in each syllable will also support learning.

1. Tell your Learner that they are going to make words with two syllables.
   - Say the first word: **picnic**
   - Repeat **picnic** and tap out each chunk (syllable) on the table as you say it: **pic/nic** (2 syllables).
   - Point to the first syllable in the box on the Learner page and say: **pic**. Point to the second syllable **nic** in the box and say **nic**.
   - Write **nic** in the box and then the whole word **picnic** (done for you).

2. Read the second word to your Learner: **into**. Ask your Learner to tap out the syllables: **in/to** (2 syllables)
   - Ask your Learner to say the word and point to the box with the syllable **in.**
   - Ask your Learner to find and point to the syllable **to** which will complete the word **into**.
   - Write **to** in the box and then write the whole word.
   - Ask your Learner to say the whole word again.
   - Repeat the same process for each of the other words.
   - Point out that some syllables are words in their own right, such as **in/to** and **up/set**, but have a different meaning when they are put together to make a longer word.

Notes:

Listen and point
Make longer words

| to | ~~nic~~ | ish | nap | set | tim | sack | net |

1. pic → nic = **picnic**

2. in → ___ = _____

3. vic → ___ = _____

4. up → ___ = _____

5. ruck → ___ = _____

6. fin → ___ = _____

7. kid → ___ = _____

8. mag → ___ = _____

Read and check
Learners read two-syllable words

1. On the Learner page use a piece of paper or your finger to cover up the second chunk (syllable) of each word.
   - Read the first syllable **cred** in the example word and then move the paper/finger, along to read **it**.
   - Blend the two syllables to read the whole word **credit**.
   - Do the same with the word **punish** in the grid.

2. Ask your Learner to read each word in the grid.
   - Ask them to read one chunk (syllable) at a time and then the whole word.
   - Tick all the words they get right. Leave the others blank.

3. When your Learner has finished, go over any words that have not been ticked.
   - Read each word chunk by chunk (sound out each letter if necessary) and then ask your Learner to read the whole word again.

4. Make a note of any words that are still a problem in the Notes box.
   - Go over these words again once or twice.
   - If any words remain a problem, or take two or three tries to get right, add them to the blank column on page 157.

Tip:

Notes:

Example word: **cred it**   **credit**

		✓
pun ish	punish	
lim it	limit	
cab in	cabin	
rap id	rapid	
hand bag	handbag	
con test	contest	
him self	himself	
prof it	profit	
sun set	sunset	
prob lem	problem	

Read and check

Learners read two-syllable words using the **vowel/sound/break** method

1. Remind your Learner that longer words can be broken up into smaller chunks (syllables).
- Syllables can be tapped out as the word is spoken.
- Every syllable has a vowel.

2. Show your Learner how to use the **vowel/sound/break method** with the word **helmet: hel/met**
- Look for the first vowel **e** and the letter sound that follows it. **This is where the syllable break is made**.
- Mark this break with a forward slash **/** and then read the whole word.

3. Read each word in the grid. Ask your Learner to find the vowel and the letter sound after it and then mark in the syllable break with a forward slash. The first two are done.
- Ask your Learner to use the vowel/sound/break method to read each word. Help them to blend the two syllables together to read the whole word.
- Tick those they mark up and read correctly.
- Make a note of any words that are a problem in the Notes box. Go over them again once or twice.
- If any words remain a problem after two or three tries, add them to the blank column on page 157.

Tip: Your Learner may find it helpful to cover the second syllable with their finger or a piece of paper.

Notes:

Example word: **helmet   hel/met**

		✓
im/pact	impact	
dras/tic	drastic	
into	into	
index	index	
flagship	flagship	
forward	forward	
garden	garden	
laptop	laptop	
finish	finish	

		✓
content	content	
upon	upon	
intend	intend	
husband	husband	
expand	expand	
handbag	handbag	
fantastic	fantastic	
himself	himself	
sunset	sunset	

Text and check
Learners read sentences with two-syllable words

1. Tell your Learner that the words in blue on the Learner page are all two-syllable words. Remember the vowel/sound/break rule.

2. Ask your Learner to read the sentences on the Learner page.
   • Support your Learner if they need it to pronounce words with two syllables. Say the whole word for them and ask them to repeat it.
   • Tick all the sentences they get right. Leave the others blank.

3. Go over sentences that have not been ticked.
   • Underline any errors in each sentence.
   • Read them to your Learner.
   • Ask your Learner to read the sentence again and tick the ones they get right.

4. Make a note of any words that are still a problem in the Notes box. Go over these words once or twice.

5. If any words remain a problem, or take two or three tries to get right, add them to the Parking page (page 167).

Tip: Remind your Learner they can cover up the second syllable if it helps – or you could do this for them.

Notes:

	✓
It is not a problem if I can get it.	
She was upset and felt sick.	
The fox crept into the dustbin.	
I will finish this and then get his lunch.	
The man fed the robin from his hand.	
The scrap fell off the back of the pickup truck.	
She has such bad habits.	
The man was unwell.	
The log cabin was lit up.	
He was left to do the job himself.	

Read and check

Learners practise reading two-syllable words

1. On the Learner page use a piece of paper or your finger to cover up the second chunk (syllable) of each word.
   - Read the first syllable **pan** in the example word and then move the paper/finger, along to read **ic**.
   - Blend the two syllables to read the whole word **panic**.

2. Ask your Learner to read all the words in the grid by reading one chunk at a time and then the whole word.
   - Tick all the words they get right. Leave the others blank.

3. When your Learner has finished, go over any words that have not been ticked.
   - Read each word chunk by chunk (sound out each letter if necessary) and then read the whole word again.
   - Make a note of any words that are still a problem in the Notes box below. Go over them again once or twice.
   - If any words remain a problem after two or three tries, add them to the Parking page (page 167).

Tip:

Notes:

Read and check
Check that you can read longer words

Example word: **pan/ic   panic**

	✓
van/ish vanish	
un/well unwell	
kid/nap kidnap	
dust/bin dustbin	
chil/dren children	
com/ic comic	
fran/tic frantic	
vic/tim victim	
ex/it exit	
un/til until	

Words from page 151	✓

Words from page 153	✓

157

Text and check

Learners read sentences with two-syllable words

1. Tell your Learner that the words in blue on the Learner page are all two-syllable words.

2. Ask your Learner to read the sentences on the Learner page.
   - Give support if needed to pronounce words with two syllables. Say the whole word and ask your Learner to repeat it after you.
   - Tick all the sentences they get right. Leave the others blank.

3. Go over sentences that have not been ticked.
   - Underline any errors in each sentence.
   - Read them to your Learner.
   - Ask your Learner to read the sentence again and tick the ones they get right.

4. Make a note of any words that are still a problem in the Notes box. Go over these words once or twice.

5. If any words remain a problem, or take two or three tries to get right, add them to the Parking page (page 167).

Tip: Use a finger or piece of paper to cover the second syllable if this helps.

Notes:

	✓
This is not the exit.	
The ship sank but he did not panic.	
The lad is unwell.	
The children got on the bus.	
The dustbin had no lid.	
The man was a kidnap victim.	
She lost her handbag and was frantic.	
The comic was fun but the rest of the act was bad.	
I will hang on until you finish.	

Spot the words

Learners search to find the Sight Words: **could**, **would**, **there**, **day**, **don't**, and **her**

1. Read the words **could**, **would**, **there**, **day**, **don't** and **her** on the Learner page to your Learner.
   - Point out that **could** and **would** both have the same ending **ould**.
   - Remind your Learner that all these words are Sight Words and are therefore not sounded out.
   - Ask your Learner to read the words.
   - Read them again if needed until your Learner is confident at reading them.

2. Ask your Learner to look at the words in the small boxes on the Learner page and find the word **could**.
   - Tick the word each time they find it. (There are 2.) Write the number down on the notepad.

3. Now ask your Learner to search the small boxes on the Learner page for each of the other words **would** (3), **there** (4), **day** (3), **don't** (4), **her** (4). Write the numbers down on the notepad.

Tip: If your Learner asks about the apostrophe in **don't** tell them not to worry about it now as it will be covered in detail later on in Turning Pages.

Notes:

could   would   there   day   don't   her

day

could

would

there

don't

would

her

there

would

don't

don't

her

her

could

there

could

would _____

would _____

there _____

day _____

don't _____

her _____

don't

her

day

don't

day

there

Read and check

Learners practise reading Sight Words learned so far

1. Tell your Learner that this is an opportunity for them to practise reading all the Sight Words they have learned so far.
  • Point out that some of the words have a capital letter.

2. Ask your Learner to read each word in the grid.
  • Tick all the words they get right and leave the others blank.

3. When your Learner has finished, go over any words that have not been ticked.
  • Read them to your Learner (do not sound them out).
  • Ask your Learner to read them again and tick the ones they get right.

4. If any words remain a problem, or take two or three tries to get right, write them in the Notes box and do 'Look and Say, Copy and Say' (as you do on the Parking page) until your Learner is confident.

Tip:

Notes:

Read and check
Check that you can read these Sight Words

	✓
there	
could	
would	
day	
out	
Her	
time	
we	
no	
about	
do	
could	
me	
they	
my	
day	
there	
are	

	✓
for	
be	
have	
of	
don't	
all	
what	
I	
she	
you	
I'm	
was	
have	
go	
Don't	
the	
put	
he	

Text and check

Learners read sentences using Sight Words and two-syllable words

1. Ask your Learner if they can read the Sight Words **could**, **would**, **there**, **day**, **don't** and **her**.
   • Remind them to read them as whole words and not by sounding them out.

2. Ask your Learner to read the sentences on the Learner page.
   • Tick all the sentences they get right. Leave the others blank.

3. Go over any sentences that have not been ticked.
   • Underline any errors in each sentence.
   • Read them to your Learner.
   • Ask your Learner to read the sentences again and to tick the ones they get right.

4. Make a note of any words that are a problem in the Notes box. Go over these once or twice.

5. If any words remain a problem, or take two or three tries to get right, add them to the Parking page (page 167).

Tip: Ask some questions about the sentences to check their understanding, such as: Where could her dad go with the kids? and What was not a good idea to wear for the picnic?

Notes:

| could | would | there | day | don't | her |

	✓
I could be there with you the next day.	
Don't put the rubbish there.	
There would be time for you to get there.	
Her dad could go to the film with the kids.	
We don't expect to finish on time.	
That was a bad day for me.	
There is not much to do.	
Don't let the dog out.	
She would be glad if he could get well.	
I'm there for her in the day time.	
I would not go to the picnic in that dress.	

Parking page

Use the page opposite to note down any sounds or words you have come across so far in the manual that your Learner needs to practise again. Do this activity when you have completed all the other activities.

1. Write the words in the first (Park) column as you come across them in the manual.

2. When you and your Learner get to this page:
- Take **one** word at a time.
- Read it to your Learner and sound it out. Note: Sight Words are **not** sounded out.
- Ask your Learner to read the word.
- Ask your Learner to copy and say it.
- Tick it if it's right.
- Repeat the process with the same word: Copy and Say, Copy and Say until they are confident with it. Repeat on a new row if needed.

3. Repeat the 'Look and Say, Copy and Say' process with all the other words in the Park column.
- If your Learner continues to struggle with a word, make sure they know what the word means and try putting it into sentences for them.

Tip:

Notes:

Parking page

Park. Look and Say	✓

Copy and Say	✓

Copy and Say	✓

Copy and Say	✓

Parking page

Use the page opposite to note down any more words your Learner needs to practise again. Treat in the same way as outlined on the previous Parking page.

Tip:

Notes:

Park. Look and Say	✓	Copy and Say	✓	Copy and Say	✓	Copy and Say	✓

Progress check

Explain to your Learner that the end of the first manual is a good point in Turning Pages to see how things are going and to check that they are confident with what they have learned so far.

Ask your Learner to read each word in the Progress check.
• Tick everything they get right.
• Leave blank any words that your Learner cannot read.
• Use the Turning Pages Reading Levels to show your Learner how much they have achieved.
• Keep a note of any words or letter sounds they are not confident with. Your Learner can practise them at the beginning of the next session.

Turning Pages Reading Levels

All or most of the words sounded out correctly, including the end sounds *tch*, *ng*, *nk* and *nd*. (No more than 10 errors.)	**TP Level 1.7**
All or most of the two-syllable words read correctly. (No more than 10 errors.)	**TP Level 1.8**

Tip:

Notes:

Read and tick all the words you know

	✓
just	
help	
mask	
belt	
tent	
lost	
gust	
went	
gift	
milk	
cost	
pant	
quick	

	✓
zest	
lump	
fetch	
duck	
song	
rash	
with	
band	
self	
film	
lisp	
toss	
weld	

	✓
swift	
blotch	
chest	
stand	
clutch	
drank	
cloth	
split	
thump	
lunch	
shelf	
frost	
bring	

Two-syllable words	✓
kidnap	
upset	
rucksack	
finish	
into	
victim	
limit	
rapid	
punish	
handbag	
himself	
problem	
cabin	

Two-syllable words	✓
sunset	
contest	
frantic	
children	
dustbin	
vanish	
unwell	
profit	
exit	
comic	
until	
panic	
tablet	

TP Level 1.7

TP Level 1.8

Turning Pages Reading Levels

1. Ask your Learner to read each word and sentence in this part of the Progress check.

2. Tick everything they get right and leave the others blank.

All or most of the Sight Words read correctly. (No more than 5 errors.)	**TP Level 1.9**
All or most of the words in the sentences read correctly. (No more than 5 errors.)	**TP Level 2.0**

If your Learner makes more than 15 errors overall (in both words and sentences) you will need to go over the relevant activities again and spend some more time practising with the Turning Pages reading books. When you have done this, try the Progress check again.

If your Learner continues to have problems they may need specialist help.

Tip:

Notes:

Progress check

Read and tick all the Sight Words you know

	✓
the	
could	
was	
put	
he	
to	
you	
out	

	✓
have	
for	
she	
do	
are	
time	
me	
day	

	✓
no	
would	
of	
there	
we	
they	
all	
don't	

	✓
I'm	
my	
go	
I	
what	
be	
about	
her	

TP Level 1.9 ☐

Read these sentences

	✓
She put her handbag on the shelf.	
The clutch on the van could be a problem.	
I'm off to fetch the children.	
He had to limit himself to soft drinks.	
Could you put the dustbin out for the bin men?	
They would help me if I ask them to.	
I don't go out on Sunday.	

TP Level 2.0 ☐

The Turning Pages Reading Levels show your Learner what they have achieved.

Congratulate them and explain what each level means.

Ask your Learner if there any letters or words that they would like to go over again. Make a note of them below.

Go over them before moving on to the next manual.

 Your Learner has achieved the skills to read the dark blue Turning Pages reading books coded Level 2.0

Tip:

Notes:

Congratulations!

You are now reading words with two syllables, more Sight Words and some short sentences.

You are now reading at **TP Level 2.0**.

In the next (light blue) manual we are going to look at:
- More four and five-letter words
- Other vowel sounds
- More Sight Words